Hierarchy Theory

THE INTERNATIONAL LIBRARY OF
SYSTEMS THEORY AND PHILOSOPHY
Edited by Ervin Laszlo

THE SYSTEMS VIEW OF THE WORLD
*The Natural Philosophy of the New
Developments in the Sciences*
by Ervin Laszlo

GENERAL SYSTEMS THEORY
Foundations—Development—Applications
by Ludwig von Bertalanffy

ROBOTS, MEN AND MINDS
Psychology in the Modern World
by Ludwig von Bertalanffy

THE RELEVANCE OF GENERAL SYSTEMS THEORY
*Papers Presented to Ludwig von Bertalanffy
on His Seventieth Birthday*
Edited by Ervin Laszlo

HIERARCHY THEORY
The Challenge of Complex Systems
Edited by H. H. Pattee

Further volumes in preparation

HIERARCHY THEORY

The Challenge of Complex Systems

EDITED BY

HOWARD H. PATTEE

GEORGE BRAZILLER   *New York*

Standard Book Number: 0-8076-0674-x, cloth
                      0-8076-0673-1, paper
Library of Congress Catalog Card Number: 72–93477
First Printing
Printed in the United States of America

Foreword

SEVERAL years ago, we in the Smithsonian Institution began thinking of ways to reawaken some of the interest in the connections between the physical and biological sciences in the tradition of our first Secretary, Dr. Joseph Henry. We agreed that it would be useful to build more bridges between these basic disciplines since the bridges already established have proved so successful, particularly in molecular biology and biophysics. The discussions which followed led to the conclusion that a common general problem of the two sciences is in how each discerns the relationship between parts and wholes. The physicist has a tradition of analytical thinking, explaining wholes in terms of smaller and smaller parts, while the biologist has more often worked in the opposite direction, from cells to tissues to whole animals, populations, and ecosystems. We recognized that while the analytical approach has been the most successfully developed, it is the problems of synthesis and control of very complex systems which now appear to be the most serious for our own survival.

To put these ideas into practice we were fortunate to obtain the support of the Office of Naval Research who cosponsored this series with the Smithsonian Institution. We are indebted to Mr. E. A. Edelsack of the Office of Naval Research and Dr. Helen Hayes of the Smithsonian Institution for much of the preliminary planning and arrangements. We are also most grateful to Dr. Howard Pattee who became interested in developing the series and who has done much of the work in obtaining our distinguished authors.

We hope that this series of papers will help stimulate a deeper interest in complex systems and hierarchy theory, not only in the fields of physics and biology, but in the more difficult areas of social, political and environmental systems where so many of our immediate problems lie.

SIDNEY GALLER

Contents

Hierarchy Theory

Preface

WE are well into a decade in which man can no longer evade the responsibility for his own survival. This is not a question of survival over geological or evolutionary time spans. It is a question of survival of his children and grandchildren in a society dominated by increasingly complex local constraints, but lacking stability and rational control.

It is a central lesson of biological evolution that increasing complexity of organization is always accompanied by new levels of hierarchical controls. The loss of these controls at any level is usually malignant for the organization under that level. Furthermore, our experience with many different types of complex systems, both natural and artificial, warns us that loss of hierarchical controls often results in sudden and catastrophic failure. Simple tools may wear out slowly and predictably, but as systems grow in size and complexity they reach a limit where a new level of hierarchical control is necessary if the system is to function reliably.

This is common knowledge to administrators, industrial managers, systems engineers, and to anyone who has successfully operated a complex organization, but all too often this knowledge has only come from trial and error type of experience. The theory and understanding of complex hierarchical systems is still in a rudimentary state.

This book explores the nature of hierarchical organization from different points of view. The aim is to give a broad perspective of the problem in non-technical language. The contributors agree that the problems of hierarchical organization are of universal and fundamental significance, and that we must learn much more about their origin and evolution if we are to claim any abilities to rationally control the complexities of survival which we now face.

In the first paper Herbert Simon shows the generality of hierarchical organizations and some of their common characteristics and reasons for existence. Although he draws examples from physics and biology, his primary interest is administrative hierarchies or "artificial" organizations. He pleads for neither a reductionist nor organismic theory, but for a better appreciation of the approximations and limits inherent in any single-level description. At each level we must learn to abstract what is most significant, for what is true in detail at a lower level does not usually give us a clear picture of the upper level.

Clifford Grobstein looks carefully at the hierarchical interfaces between several different levels of biological organization, and at the way structure and information at one level are reinterpreted at a higher level. Properties that appear to emerge in developing collections may be understood as reading a message in a new context. This context is established by the relationships in the collection, and therefore is not to be found in the detailed structures of the lower level. It is this context change in what he calls the set-superset transition that creates new hierarchical levels.

James Bonner describes some of the known requirements for the developmental process in multicellular organisms, which is the epitome of hierarchical control. Along with many other workers, Bonner finds the language of the computer well-suited to describe developmental processes, in particular the concepts of conditional tests at various stages of a program, the outcomes of which lead to different subroutines. The absolute requirement for explicitness in computer programs also points up the logical complexity of what appears at first to be relatively simple structural development.

In the fourth paper, I try to find some basic principles of hierarchical control by studying how life may have originated from the non-living physical and chemical world. This might be the simplest level of hierarchical origins, but even if it is, we have yet to see with any clarity how such integrated controls as the genetic code or developmental programs could come into being. I concur with Simon and Grobstein that a new description is required for each level, but the spontaneous origin of the natural genetic description remains a serious difficulty.

In the concluding paper, Richard Levins considers some possible origins and limitations on the complexity of evolving biological systems. He argues that a collection of interacting units will naturally evolve away from a maximum complexity of interaction; that is, away from a uniform, totally connected network. One might say that highly interrelated collections will condense into simple, persistent relations in the course of evolution. These persistent relations establish a hierarchical cluster of adaptive traits. But since networks of different relations can overlap there will appear multiple hierarchies whose dynamics will again be too complex, and which in turn will evolve new hierarchical simplifications. Thus, relational complexity is self-limiting, so that the intricacies of what does not become hierarchically organized lose significance.

These five papers were originally presented to a diverse audience with the hope of emphasizing the fundamental necessity of hierarchical control in all living organizations, as well as generating more interest and support toward solving fundamental problems of the origin and functioning of complex hierarchical organizations. The papers were not meant to be technical or comprehensive, and consequently they do not contain extensive references.

We hope these papers will stimulate some readers to look further into this vital type of problem which cannot, by its nature, be analyzed away. One place to start is the collection of papers in *Hierarchical Structures,* edited by L. L. Whyte, A. G. Wilson, and D. Wilson, American Elsevier Publishing Company, Inc., New York, 1969. This book includes a wide range of discussions of hierarchical structures and organizations, and concludes with a selected, annotated bibliography by Donna Wilson covering the concept of hierarchy in its widest sense, from physics and astronomy up through biology and sociology, to art and philosophy. The breadth of the subject can also be illustrated by comparing such recent books on hierarchy theory as *Hierarchically Organized Systems in Theory and Practice* by Paul Weiss, Hafner Publishing Company, New York 1971, which is a collection of papers at the biological, social and ecosystem levels; and *Theory of Hierarchical, Multilevel Systems* by M. D. Mesarovic, D. Macko, and Y. Takahara, Academic Press, New York, 1970, which takes a mathematical approach to engineering problems of production and control.

The purpose of this volume remains much the same as the purpose of the original lectures—to clarify relationships between parts and wholes of hierarchical systems from the perspectives of basic physics and biology. The editor of The International Library of Systems Theory and Philosophy has asked me to give further examples of hierarchical control, as well as some ideas on the directions the development of hierarchy theory may take. I have tried to do this in a postscript, and also to point out some of the fundamental problems about hierarchical control, which we must understand before we can safely predict the consequences of imposing such controls artificially on biological and social organizations.

H.P.

1

The Organization
of Complex Systems

HERBERT A. SIMON

THE Nobel Laureate Hideki Yukawa earned his prize by observing that the neutron and the proton required a strong, localized force field to hold them together in the atomic nucleus, and that this field should have the properties of a particle—the particle we now know as the pi-meson or pion. The organizers of this series of lectures, having described it as "an experiment in communication between physicists and biologists," evidently concluded that those two kinds of particles—physicists and biologists—also required a binding force to hold them in stable communication. Borrowing Yukawa's idea, they invited me—a behavioral scientist by training—to serve as the pion for the series.

Although I am neither physicist nor biologist, I cannot claim complete innocence of the subject of complex, hierarchic systems, for human administrative organizations— business firms, governments, universities, churches—to which I have devoted a considerable part of my research, are excellent examples of such systems. Since human organizations are staffed by human beings, and since human beings are biological organisms, it might be argued that my research problem is indeed biological. And since biological organisms are constructed from molecules, and those molecules from atoms, and the atoms from elementary particles—all obeying the laws of quantum mechanics—it might even be argued that research on human organizations is merely a rather baroque branch of physics.

I do not intend, however, to talk specifically about either biology or physics. The main point of my paper will be that there are properties common to a very broad class of complex systems, independently of whether those systems are physical, chemical, biological, social, or artificial. The existence of these commonalities is a matter of empirical observation; their explanation is, in a broad sense, Darwinian—they concern properties that facilitate the evolution and survival of complexity. I will leave to the other speakers in the series the specific applications of a general theory of complexity to biological phenomena.

My remarks will fall under four main headings. First, I will define what I—and I hope the other speakers in the series—mean by "hierarchy." Second, I will review briefly two extant pieces of mathematical theory about hierarchies: One has to do with the time required for their evolution, the other with the interaction of their parts. Third, I will explore some consequences of the fact that biological organisms have hierarchic structure. Fourth, I will draw implications from the hierarchies of nature for the hierarchy of the sciences.

In dealing with each topic, I will turn to two main sources of illustration and example, making my discourse into a sort of two-part fugue. On the one hand, I will draw examples from biology, and occasionally from chemistry and physics. On the other hand, I will draw examples from computer science, and specifically from the structure of computer programming languages and programs. I hope that the relation between these two sets of examples will become clear as I proceed.

Hierarchy

In discussions of the theory of complex systems, the term "hierarchy" has taken on a somewhat generalized meaning, divorced from its original denotation in human organizations of a vertical authority structure. In application to the architecture of complex systems, "hierarchy" simply means a set of Chinese boxes of a particular kind. A set of Chinese boxes usually consists of a box enclosing a second box, which, in turn, encloses a third—the recursion continuing as long as the patience of the craftsman holds out.

The Chinese boxes called "hierarchies" are a variant of that pattern. Opening any given box in a hierarchy discloses not just one new box within, but a whole small set of boxes; and opening any one of these component boxes discloses a new set in turn. While the ordinary set of Chinese boxes is a sequence, or complete ordering, of the component boxes, a hierarchy is a partial ordering—specifically, a tree.

It is a commonplace observation that nature loves hierarchies. Most of the complex systems that occur in nature find their place in one or more of four intertwined hierarchic sequences. One partial ordering of boxes starts with observable chemical substances. Analysis of these discloses sets of component molecules. Within the molecules are found atoms, within the atoms, nuclei and electrons, and finally—or is it momentarily?—within the nuclei are found elementary particles.

A second important hierarchy runs from living organisms to tissues and organs, to cells, to macromolecules, to organic compounds, to a junction with the molecules of the first hierarchy. A third, intertwined hierarchy leads from the statistics of inheritance to genes and chromosomes, to DNA, and all that.

A fourth hierarchy, not yet firmly connected with the others, leads from human societies to organizations, to small groups, to individual human beings, to cognitive programs in the central nervous system, to elementary information processes—where the junctions with the tissues and organs of neurobiology largely remain to be discovered.

In this fourth hierarchy, I have included components called "programs" and other components called "elementary information processes." Walter Pitts once referred to this system as "the hierarchy of final causes called the mind." Until about twenty-five years ago, programs and elementary information processes were to be found only as components of biological organisms. Since that time, programs and elementary information processes have been occurring with growing abundance in the artificial complex systems called digital computers. Since programs are much more readily accessible to study in their artificial than in their natural environments, we have learned enormously more about them in our generation than in all previous history. For this reason, the digital computer is taking its place alongside Drosophila, Neurospora, and bacteriophage as an experimental system of the greatest importance. It is for this reason, also, that I shall parallel my biological examples with examples drawn from computer science.

Some Theory of Hierarchy

Several theoretical results are available today on the general behavior of hierarchic systems. I wish to mention two: One providing some explanation for the frequent occurrence of hierarchies in nature, the other showing that there are certain general properties that all hierarchic systems can be expected to possess, wherever they fit in the ordering of

Chinese boxes, and whatever they are made of. I will review these two results here only briefly because I have previously treated them at some length in an essay recently reissued as the fourth chapter of my Compton Lectures at MIT, entitled "The Sciences Of The Artificial" (Cambridge, Massachusetts, MIT Press, 1969).

THE SPEED OF EVOLUTION

One can show on quite simple and general grounds that the time required for a complex system, containing k elementary components, say, to evolve by processes of natural selection from those components is very much shorter if the system is itself comprised of one or more layers of stable component subsystems than if its elementary parts are its only stable components. The mathematics of the matter is a straightforward exercise in probabilities, but the gist of it can be given even more simply in a parable.

Two watchmakers assemble fine watches, each watch containing ten thousand parts. Each watchmaker is interrupted frequently to answer the phone. The first has organized his total assembly operation into a sequence of subassemblies; each subassembly is a stable arrangement of 100 elements, and each watch, a stable arrangement of 100 subassemblies. The second watchmaker has developed no such organization. The average interval between phone interruptions is a time long enough to assemble about 150 elements. An interruption causes any set of elements that does not yet form a stable system to fall apart completely. By the time he has answered about eleven phone calls, the first watchmaker will usually have finished assembling a watch. The second watchmaker will almost never succeed in assembling one—he will

7

suffer the fate of Sisyphus: As often as he rolls the rock up the hill, it will roll down again.

It has been argued on information-theoretic grounds—or, what amounts to the same thing, on thermodynamic grounds—that organisms are highly improbable arrangements of matter; so improbable, in fact, that there has hardly been time enough, since the Earth's creation, for them to evolve. The calculation on which this argument is based does not take account of the hierarchic arrangement of stable subassemblies in the organisms that have actually evolved. It has erroneously used the analogy of the second, unsuccessful watchmaker; and when the first watchmaker is substituted for him, the times required are reduced to much more plausible magnitudes.

Specifically, on the simplest assumptions, the mathematical model shows that if a system of k elementary components is built up in a many-level hierarchy, and s components, on the average, combine at any level into a component at the next higher level, then the expected time of evolution for the whole system will be proportional to the logarithm to base s of k. In such a hierarchy, the time required for systems containing, say, 10^{25} atoms to evolve from systems containing 10^{23} atoms would be the same as the time required for systems containing 10^3 atoms to evolve from systems containing 10 atoms. The form of the generalization is interesting, in that it describes a relation between two levels of a system that is independent of absolute level.

We conclude that hierarchies will evolve much more rapidly from elementary constituents than will non-hierarchic systems containing the same number of elements. Hence, almost all the very large systems will have hierarchic organization. And this is what we do, in fact, observe in nature.

NEAR-DECOMPOSABILITY

Most interactions that occur in nature, between systems of all kinds, decrease in strength with distance. Hence, any given "particle" has most of its strong interactions with nearby particles. As a result, a system is likely to behave either as made up of a collection of localized subsystems or to form a more or less uniform "tissue" of equally strong interactions. An example of the former would be a system of molecules; an example of the latter would be a crystal or a piece of rock. Systems of the former kind are, again, hierarchies.

Thus, protons and neutrons of the atomic nucleus interact strongly through the pion fields, which dispose of energies of some 140 million electron volts each. The covalent bonds that hold molecules together, on the other hand, involve energies only on the order of 5 electron volts. And the bonds that account for the tertiary structure of large macromolecules, hence for their biological activity, involve energies another order of magnitude smaller—around one-half of an electron volt. It is precisely this sharp gradation in bond strengths at successive levels that causes the system to appear hierarchic and to behave so. As Melvin Calvin has put it: "This is one of the fundamental things we have to teach freshmen: What is the difference between an atom and a molecule? An atom interacts at one energy level and molecules interact at the other, and that is how we tell the difference." (See Diane M. Ramsey, ed. 1967)

Suppose we were to write down and solve the equations describing the behavior of a hierarchic system having n degrees of freedom. We would obtain n frequencies, not necessarily all distinct, in terms of which we could describe the dynamic behavior. We could arrange these frequencies in a

sequence, beginning with the lowest frequencies corresponding to the slowest oscillations, and going down through
medium-range frequencies, to very high frequencies at the
end of the list. As is well known, in the case of the physical
system I described a moment ago—a system of macromolecules—Planck's Law prescribes a strict proportional-
ity between bond energies and the associated frequencies.

If we now observe the behavior of the system over a total
time span, T, and our observational techniques do not allow
us to detect changes during time intervals shorter than τ, we
can break the sequence of characteristic frequencies into
three parts: (1) low frequencies, much less than $1/T$; (2)
middle-range frequencies; and (3) high frequencies, greater
than $1/\tau$. Motions of the system determined by the low-
frequency modes will be so slow that we will not observe
them—they will be replaced by constants.

Motions of the system determined by the high frequency
modes will control, for the reasons already given, the internal
interactions of the components of the lower level subsystems
in the hierarchy, but will not be involved in the interactions
among those subsystems. Moreover, these motions will be so
rapid that the corresponding subsystems will appear always
to be in equilibrium and most of their internal degrees of
freedom will vanish. In their relations with each other, the
several subsystems will behave like rigid bodies, so to speak.

The middle band of frequencies, which remains after we
have eliminated the very high and very low frequencies, will
determine the observable dynamics of the system under
study—the dynamics of interaction of the major subsystems.
As we have seen, these dynamics will be nearly independent
of the detail of the internal structure of the subsystems,
which will never be observed far from equilibrium. Hence,

we can build a theory of the system at the level of dynamics that is observable, in ignorance of the detailed structure or dynamics at the next level down, and ignore the very slow interactions at the next level up. The goodness of our approximation will depend only on the sharpness of the separation of the high frequencies from the middle-range frequencies, and of the middle-range frequencies from the low frequencies. We will, of course, want to select the boundaries so as to make that separation as sharp as possible. I will have a little more to say about the relation between the layered structure of natural phenomena and the layered structure of theories.

Systems with the sorts of dynamic properties that I have just described are called "nearly-decomposable" or sometimes "nearly completely decomposable" systems. A rigorous mathematical basis exists for reaching the conclusions I have just stated about such systems, but I think our intuitions will suffice for present purposes. (See Ando et al., 1963.)

Hierarchies in Computing Systems

So far I have used natural systems as my examples of hierarchies. I could as well have used modern computing systems and their behavior. I should now like to describe a computer program called EPAM with which I am familiar. EPAM simulates human laboratory subjects in certain simple learning tasks, but just what it does is of no concern to us here. What is important is that it is a large, complex computer program.

EPAM consists of lists of instructions organized as "routines." It is written in a computer programming language called IPL-V, to which I will return in a moment. The instructions—there are about 3,000—are of two kinds: (1) primitive instructions, corresponding to a fixed, basic set of IPL-V instructions, and (2) higher-level instructions. Whenever I write an IPL-V routine consisting of a list of primitive instructions, I can give that routine a name. I can then use that name just as though it were an instruction—a higher-level instruction—in any other routine I wish to write. Whenever the system, during execution, encounters such a higher level instruction, it simply executes the subroutine that the instruction names. There is no limit to the allowable number of levels of subroutines, and at various points EPAM is five or even ten levels deep.

But that is not all. The IPL-V primitives, in terms of which the EPAM routines are ultimately defined, are themselves not very primitive. They correspond, in fact, to routines—some of them fairly complex—written in the instruction language of the particular kind of computer on which EPAM is to be run. For each distinct machine there must be a translation of IPL-V into the language of that machine; but the behavior of EPAM is substantially independent of that translation and indifferent to what machine it is run on. We can say that EPAM has a "meaning" that is independent of the particular machine language in which it is expressed.

We are still far from having probed the bottom levels of our hierarchy. Having reached the level of machine instructions, we can analyse how these instructions are realized in the logical organization of the computer itself. The study of that logical organization leads, in turn, to lower hierarchic levels, where we first encounter the actual physical devices that implement the behavior and the actual physical laws that govern those devices. Just as the same language—for example, IPL-V—can be implemented on vastly different computers (more than a dozen translations exist today), so the same computer design, at the logical level, can be implemented with entirely different hardware devices. From a programming standpoint, the IBM 709 and the IBM 7090 were almost identical machines, although the former made extensive use of vacuum tubes, while the latter was a solid-state system. From a physical standpoint, they were radically different machines.

The system I have described is a nearly-decomposable system. Its highest frequencies are those associated with the physical components of the computer—nowadays, microsecond or nanosecond frequencies. Frequencies associated with the logical organization of the machine and its machine instructions might be, for a fairly fast machine, say, in the range of ten microseconds. IPL-V instructions are executed at millisecond rates (one or two orders of magnitude slower than machine instructions). Some of the higher-level routines of EPAM take seconds to execute—even on a fast modern computer, EPAM requires several seconds to memorize a nonsense syllable.

Now just as we can reach an approximate understanding of a physical system at the level of chemical reactions, ignoring what is going on within the atoms and nuclei, so we can reach an approximate understanding of EPAM by considering only a few of the highest levels of the program, not going down even to IPL-V primitives, much less to machine language, logical design, or computer physics. As a matter of fact, since IPL-V translators are explicitly constructed to make behavior machine-independent, we should be able to describe EPAM *exactly* (apart from some speed parameters) in terms of IPL-V. How much accuracy we lose in disregarding all but the high-level routines depends on how carefully we have sealed off each level from those below.

What do I mean by "sealing off"? Each year when I fill out my income tax form, I am instructed to perform certain additions and subtractions, and even a few multiplications. I am told where to find the operands and where to enter the sum, difference, or product. Later, the Internal Revenue Service audits my return, and if I have made a mistake—as I sometimes do—corrects it. So the IRS can tell whether I have done the arithmetic correctly, but it cannot tell *how* I did it—what subroutine I use to define "addition" or "multiplication." Perhaps I multiply with paper and pencil, from right to left, or from left to right; perhaps I do it in my head, or on a desk calculator, or on my university's computer; perhaps my wife does it. The only communication between my arithmetic routines and the IRS's auditing routines is through the inputs and outputs of my processes; the processes themselves are immune from scrutiny.

When I multiply two four-digit numbers together, I have to keep the multiplier and multiplicand in memory or on paper. Then I have to store temporarily the four partial products—four or five digits each. When I am done, I have to retain only the seven or eight digits of the final product. The unobservability (to the IRS) of the intermediate results that I create, but hold only temporarily, is precisely analogous to the unobservability of the high-frequency dynamics of a hierarchic system, the disequilibrium dynamics of the smallest components. All of this detail is simply irrelevant to the lower-frequency interactions among the larger segments. No matter which of several processes I use to obtain the product, and which intermediate results I obtain *en route,* the final information I obtain and pass on to other routines is the same. Hence, hierarchy is associated with a very fundamental form of parsimony of interactions. The art of subroutining, in writing complex computer programs, consists in discovering the points of cleavage at which the least information needs to be passed from one subroutine to another.

LOOSE HORIZONTAL COUPLING

In describing the behavior of nearly-decomposable systems, I emphasized "vertical" separation—the segregation of the low-frequency from the high-frequency dynamics. The last examples suggest that the theory of near-decomposability can be extended to say something about the horizontal relations among subsystems at the *same* hierarchic level.

Consider, again, the frequencies of a nearly-decomposable system arranged in order from low to high. We now observe the behavior of the system much more microscopically than we did before, so that we need consider only the roots of frequency greater than $1/\tau$. This is equivalent to ignoring the weak interactions among the subsystems of the nearly-decomposable system and treating the subsystems as completely decoupled from one another. But then we can take the remaining high-frequency roots and assign them to their respective subsystems. Particular frequencies describe the behavior of particular subsystems.

Returning to our original system, we see that the frequencies describing its dynamics can be *partially* ordered, and each subset of frequencies in the partial ordering (formally, an equivalence class at some particular level of the ordering) can be associated with a specific subsystem in the partial ordering of system components. There will be, essentially, an isomorphism between the hierarchy of subsystems and the hierarchy of equivalence classes of frequencies describing the system, and particular frequencies will "belong" to particular subsystems.

To a first approximation, the behavior of any given subsystem will depend only on the frequencies belonging to it, together with the lower frequencies belonging to systems at higher levels of the hierarchy. It will be independent of the frequencies associated with other subsystems at the same or lower levels of the hierarchy. (I am sorry that high "frequencies" correspond to low "levels," but it can't be helped.)

The loose horizontal coupling of the components of hierarchic systems has great importance for evolutionary processes just as the loose vertical coupling does. The loose vertical coupling permits the stable subassemblies to be treated as simple givens, whose dynamic behavior is irrelevant to assembling the larger structures, only their equilibrium properties affecting system behavior at the higher levels.

The loose horizontal coupling permits each subassembly to operate dynamically in independence of the detail of the others; only the inputs it requires and the outputs it produces are relevant for the larger aspects of system behavior. In programming terms, it is permissible to improve the system by modifying any one of the subroutines, provided that the subroutine's inputs and outputs are not altered.

When the same outputs can be obtained from the same inputs by two or more different paths, we usually speak of "functional equivalence." Functional equivalence, of course, is not peculiar to computer programs, for it occurs frequently in natural phenomena. In chemical reactions, for example, isotopic variants of atoms of the elements are usually functionally equivalent—as long as two atoms present to the surrounding environment the same configuration of outer-shell electrons and differ only slightly in atomic weight, their chemical behaviors are almost indistinguishable.

In biological systems, innumerable examples of functional equivalence are provided by multiple reaction pathways. The equivalence can refer to the reaction itself—for example, the two pathways for synthesis of lysine, one employed by some fungi and euglenids, the others by most plants. Alternatively, the equivalence can refer to the enzymic apparatus controlling the reaction—for example, the wide variety of chemically distinguishable protein molecules that serve as functionally equivalent hemoglobins, both among different species and even in a single species.

The various functional equivalents may, of course, vary widely in their metabolic efficiency, and their relative efficiencies may depend on environmental circumstances as well —horse hemoglobin seems to work better for horses and human hemoglobin for people, although perhaps that is only for immunological reasons. But, of course, it is precisely because they may vary in efficiency that functional equivalents have significance for natural selection. Functional equivalence permits mutation and natural selection to go on in particular subsystems without requiring synchronous changes in all the other systems that make up the total organism.

The loose horizontal coupling of components can be observed at all levels of hierarchic structures. Thus, a mammal's circulatory system is loosely coupled to other systems. It receives oxygen from the respiratory system and nutrients from the digestive system. It delivers these to the muscles, say, from which it receives carbon dioxide, and other wastes. These it delivers, in turn, to lungs and kidneys, and so on.

17

Just how the circulatory system accomplishes these tasks is of no concern, so to speak, to the other systems, as long as it does accomplish them. Appropriate evolutionary changes may take place in any one of these systems without necessarily, or immediately, disturbing the others. Natural selection may improve a horse's locomotion without necessarily changing his digestion, although changes in the metabolic rates associated with one subsystem may, on a longer time scale, bring about natural selection of new adaptations of other subsystems.

The same kind of argument as that used to show that nearly-decomposable systems will evolve more rapidly than others can be used to demonstrate that the advantage in adaptation will be increased if different components of the organism are coupled to different components of the environment. The point is most easily shown by analogy with problem solving efficiency.

Consider the problem of cracking a safe that has 10 dials, each with 10 possible settings. To find the combination by trial and error would require, on the average, testing half the total number of possible settings—half of 10^{10}, or 5 billion. If each dial emits a faint click when it is set to the correct number, the safe-cracking job becomes trivially simple. Now, on average, only $5 \times 10 = 50$ settings will have to be tried.

PRODUCTION SYSTEMS

The loose horizontal coupling of subsystems can be exploited in another way: to make each subsystem independent of the exact timing of the operation of the others. If subsystem B depends upon subsystem A only for a certain substance, then B can be made independent of fluctuations in A's production by maintaining a buffer inventory of the substance upon which B can draw. The storage of fat is a well-known and important biological example of this principle. Buffer inventories permit many interdependent processes to operate in parallel, at fluctuating rates and under only feed-back control—as in the familiar mechanism by which the inventory of the substance produced by the last enzyme in a chain inhibits the activity of the first enzyme.

Most digital computers are organized, more or less, as serial one-process-at-a-time devices. The idea of loosely coupling their processes in the way just described can be employed to simulate parallel systems. To do this each routine is written as a "production" in two parts: The first part tests for the presence or absence of certain conditions; if and only if the conditions are satisfied, the second part carries out its characteristic process. Clearly, there is a close logical relation between such productions and the operons of molecular genetics. If one wanted to write a computer simulation of operons, one would represent them by productions. Because their components are so loosely coupled, production systems are much more easily modified, component by component, than are computer programs written as more traditional sub-routine structures. As a result, complex programs are increasingly being organized in this form.

Alphabets

The flexibility of coupling among subsystems can be further enhanced by limiting the variety of different kinds of components that are incorporated in the larger systems. When the numerous component elements (called "tokens") of the subsystems of a hierarchy all belong to a small number of basic types, we call this set of types an "alphabet." A common milk protein contains 5,941 "tokens"—atoms. All of these atoms belong to the five elements—types C, H, O, N, and S. These five types are drawn from the 92-letter alphabet of natural elements.

The alphabet of primitive instructions in IPL-V is more baroque than the atomic alphabet. It contains about 150 instructions, but if we treat certain similar instructions as isotopes, the number remaining is not far from the number of elements. As Turing and others have shown, a computing system—even a completely general one—can get along with a far smaller alphabet than that. In fact, about five instructions like "write," "erase," "move left," "move right," and "test and branch" will suffice for complete generality. It is convenient and efficient, but not logically necessary, for computer instruction codes to contain more operations than these.

Two alphabets have supreme importance for biology: The alphabet of twenty-odd amino acids, and the alphabet of four (or five) nucleic acids. I will confine my remarks largely to the former, for we know today how the one can be translated into the other.

ALPHABETS, LANGUAGES, AND PROGRAMS

Not every level in a hierarchic structure is characterized by a small alphabet of components. There are only 92 natural elements, but innumerable molecules at the next level up; there are only about 20 amino acids, but innumerable protein molecules. There are only 150 primitive IPL-V instructions, but innumerable routines written in terms of them—at least thousands. What significance can we attach to the fact that only certain hierarchic levels are alphabetic?

We must distinguish between alphabets and languages, on the one hand, and programs or messages, on the other. Alphabets and languages are systems that provide a potentiality for communicating any of a large number of programs or messages. They consist of elements, and rules for the combination of the elements into messages. We may regard alphabets simply as those languages that are based on small numbers of different elements (as distinct, for example, from natural languages, which typically contain hundreds of thousands of morphemes or words).

Members of a single organization may share a set of common messages—standard operating procedures, say. Interaction throughout a language community takes place by means of a common language, messages being constructed and transmitted as needed. Alphabets, because of their restricted set of elements, are even shared across the boundaries of language communities. Most of the Western European languages use the Roman alphabet.

If we knew in advance just what messages were to be sent, we could always find a special encoding that would be more efficient than constructing the messages from a general-purpose language. If we knew in advance the subject of the messages, a lexicon could provide a more efficient encoding of messages than is provided by the combinations of a small alphabet. The "inventory" of elements we would have to keep on hand would be much greater, however, for the lexicon than for the alphabet.

To realize its potential advantages for communication, a language should have these characteristics: (1) sufficient variety in its primitive processes so that no meaning is absolutely excluded from expression, and (2) sufficient flexibility in its rules of combination so that any nuance can be expressed by building up composite structures. What is required of the amino acids, and of the nucleic acids, is that they provide sufficient variety so that their combinations, proteins, and chromosomes, respectively, can perform all of the basic kinds of chemical functions that need to be performed in the cell.

This does not explain, however, why the nucleic acid and amino acid languages are based on alphabets. If this characteristic has significance for evolutionary success, the significance appears to be different in the two cases. What is needed in the genetic case is a simple code that is isomorphic to the set of amino acids—hence nothing is to be gained from a large alphabet. But what about the amino acids themselves?

An organism can only survive in an environment containing appropriate nutrient matter. Unless it can control that environment, or unless the environment is controlled beneficiently by a higher-level system, it cannot rely on finding in the environment highly particular substances. We would expect alphabetic languages to be prominent in communication at subsystem boundaries where each subsystem experiences considerable uncertainty as to what it will find in its environment—where it cannot count on the environment to provide inputs tailored to its exact needs.

(I may observe that manufacturing concerns behave in exactly the same way. They tend to hold their in-process inventories in the form of generalized intermediate products that are capable of being formed into a variety of final products—ingots rather than special steel shapes, for example.)

It is hardly surprising, therefore, that the transactions of an organism with its environment (and even remote internal transactions via its circulatory system) are handled with an amino acid currency, and not with a protein currency. Proteins are far too specific in function, and far too closely adapted to a particular type of organism, to be exchanged satisfactorily among organisms. An amino acid molecule in the bloodstream of an animal may have come from many different sources. It may have been obtained by digestion of protein foods of various kinds; it may have been synthesized from other amino acids; it may have been hydrolyzed from proteins in the animal's own tissues. Two molecules of the same amino acid are functionally equivalent, however derived.

An organism will have access to a supply of components if it maintains itself in a broth of potential replacement parts. It would be hard-pressed—at least without cannibalism—to find such a broth of appropriate proteins.

SUMMARY: LOOSE COUPLING

Our whole discussion to this point underscores the crucial significance of hierarchic organization to the synthesis and survival of large, complex systems. To a Platonic mind, everything in the world is connected with everything else—and perhaps it is. Everything is connected, but some things are more connected than others. The world is a large matrix of interactions in which most of the entries are very close to zero, and in which, by ordering those entries according to their orders of magnitude, a distinct hierarchic structure can be discerned.

By virtue of hierarchic structure, the functional efficacy of the higher-level structures, their stability, can be made relatively independent of the detail of their microscopic components. By virtue of hierarchy, the several components on any given level can preserve a measure of independence to adapt to their special aspects of the environment without destroying their usefulness to the system.

Reduction

I will close with some remarks about reductionism and the structure of the sciences. The general tenor of these remarks should now be predictable. There are at least two versions of the concept of explanation in science. In both versions, of course, explaining a phenomenon involves reducing it to other phenomena that are, in some sense, more fundamental.

But with agreement on this point, the two concepts of explanation branch. The one concept—let me call it Laplacian—takes as its ideal the formulation of a single set of equations describing behavior at the most microscopic, the most fundamental level, from which all macrophenomena are to follow and to be deduced. No one, of course, believes that the program could actually be carried out—the equations, when written, would be far too hard to solve. In spite of that, the concept has practical consequences in the real world, for it influences some scientists' choices of research problems—their view of what is "really" fundamental.

The second concept—for lack of a better name let me call it Mendelian—takes as its ideal the formulation of laws that express the invariant relations between successive levels of hierarchic structures. It aims at discovering as many bodies of scientific law as there are pairs of successive levels—a theory of particle physics, one of atomic physics, one of molecular chemistry, one of biochemistry, and so on. Since the world of nature is a nearly-decomposable system, and since the invariant properties of a nearly-decomposable system have this layered quality, the fundamental scientific laws must take this form also.

Since, in the second view, nature is only *nearly*-decomposable, not *completely* decomposable, many of the most beautiful regularities of nature will only be approximate regularities. They will fall short of exactness because the properties of the lower-level, higher-frequency subsystems will "show through" faintly into the behavior of the higher-level, lower-frequency systems. Thus, for example, there is a fundamental truth in Prout's hypothesis—that the atomic weights of all the elements can be expressed as integers—even though we know it is not an exact truth, and know the relativistic explanation for the mass deficiency. We know the vicissitudes that Prout's hypothesis suffered: How it was discredited by the 19th century's measurement, with continually increasing accuracy, of fractional atomic weights; how it was triumphantly vindicated by the discovery of isotopes; how further increases in the accuracy of measurement put it in doubt again.

If we were to make a list of the most important, the most beautiful laws of natural science that have been discovered in the past three centuries, we would see that the vast majority of them hold only approximately, and only if we are willing to ignore details of microstructure. The pattern expressed by these laws is simply not present in the underlying, detailed Laplacian equations.

I do not want to present a one-sided case. The fact that nature is hierarchic does not mean that phenomena at several levels cannot, even in the Mendelian view, have common mechanisms. Relativistic quantum mechanics has had spectacular success in dealing with phenomena ranging all the way from the level of the atomic nucleus to the level of tertiary structure in organic molecules.

Perhaps a balanced way to state the matter is this: Suppose you decided that you wanted to understand the mysterious EPAM program that I have, without explaining, alluded to several times in this paper. I could provide you with two versions of it. One would be the IPL-V version—the form in which it was actually written—with its whole structure of routines and subroutines. If you were curious about its implementation on a computer, I could supplement the EPAM program with a listing of the program that translates IPL-V instructions into machine-language instructions for some particular machine.

Alternatively, I could provide you with a machine-language version of EPAM after the whole translation had been carried out—after it had been flattened, so to speak, and spread out in all its Laplacian detail. I don't think I need argue at length which of these two versions would provide the most parsimonious, the most meaningful, the most lawful description of EPAM. I will not even propose to you the third, and truly Laplacian possibility—of providing you with neither program, but instead, with the electromagnetic equations and boundary conditions that the computer, viewed as a physical system, would have to obey while behaving as EPAM. That would be the acme of reduction and incomprehensibility.

Notice that in my plea for a hybrid Laplacian-Mendelian approach to fundamental science I have given no defense of vitalism, nor have I alluded to the Heisenberg Uncertainty Principle. Both of these seem to me red herrings across our particular path of inquiry. Scientific knowledge is organized in levels, not because reduction in principle is impossible, but because nature is organized in levels, and the pattern at each level is most clearly discerned by abstracting from the detail of the levels far below. (The pattern of a halftone does not become clearer when we magnify it so that the individual spots of ink become visible.) And nature is organized in levels because hierarchic structures—systems of Chinese boxes—provide the most viable form for any system of even moderate complexity. I have tried in this paper to show some of the deeper reasons why this is so.

REFERENCES

Ando, A., Fisher, F. M., and Simon, H. A. 1963. *Essays on the Structure of Social Science Models.* Cambridge, Massachusetts: MIT Press.
Ramsey, Diane M., ed. 1967. *Molecular Coding Problems,* pp. 120–121. New York: New York Academy of Sciences.

2

*Hierarchical Order
and Neogenesis*

CLIFFORD GROBSTEIN

HIERARCHICAL ORDER is nowhere more striking than in biological systems. The living world as a first approximation consists of individual organisms. More sophisticated analysis shows, however, that, depending upon our purposes, the living world may be viewed as populations of organisms in higher sets called communities or ecosystems and that individual organisms may be viewed as collectives or sets of units called cells. These, in turn, may be regarded as sets of systematically ordered macromolecular complexes and as an intricate flow of energy and materials. We are therefore strongly driven to regard, as essential to our understanding of life, notions of levels of order and of hierarchical systems.

We can define hierarchical order more formally in the following terms. In common with Professor Simon I like to use Chinese boxes to convey the concept of hierarchical order (Figure 1). In its simplest sense hierarchical order refers to a complex of successively more encompassing sets. In hierarchies a given set must be described not only for itself but in terms both of what is within *it* and what it is *within*. Triangle AEG in Figure 1 consists of four subtriangles, one of which is AHJ, and it in turn consists of four subtriangles. If one were to describe fully triangle AHJ, one would say that it is a triangle which is part of a larger triangle (AEG) and that it has four triangles as its components.

We can turn this into a general statement which defines a level of order in a hierarchical system. If S is a set consisting of identifiable components A, B, C . . . N, then the components make up a level of order when they are in a determinate association R which is the sum of the relationships among the components. The set so defined is a level of order because

31

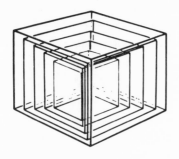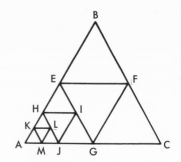

Hierarchical order in Chinese boxes and subdivided triangles. Note that the triangle ABC is made up of four identical triangles, one of which is AEG. Similarly, AEG is made up of four triangles, one of which is AHJ. This triangle, in turn, is made up of four triangles, one of which is AKM.

Figure 1. Hierarchical order in Chinese boxes and subdivided triangles. (From Grobstein, Clifford. 1965. *Strategy of life.* San Francisco: Freeman & Co.)

it has unitary properties at that level which stem not only from the properties of the components but from the particular relationships among them. The set belongs to a system which is hierarchical when the set so defined has components which also are sets and when it itself is a component in a more encompassing set. Thus in a hierarchical system each component is a set.

$$S = [A,B,C \ldots N]^R$$

where S itself is a component of a set and A, B, C and N also are comparable sets.

This general statement focuses attention on the nature of the relationships, R, and the effects of R on the properties of components and of the whole system. This is illuminating because there are at least quantitative differences between

32

living and non-living systems in the characteristics of R. For example, the nature of R might be such that the properties of individual components are little altered depending upon whether or not R obtains. Under such circumstances we may expect formation of S to be readily reversible, that is:

When S is a set containing A as a component and for a given A:

$$[A]^R = A$$
$$\text{then } S \rightleftharpoons \text{non-S}$$

Such a system may be called a simple aggregate and is illustrated by a sandpile whose grains of sand contribute to the weight, color, and shape of the pile, though the grains themselves are quite indistinguishable as to properties, whether they are within the pile or out of it. This situation clearly is not characteristic of living systems. In such systems, components are almost always different in properties depending upon the context of the system within which they operate. This functional adaptability of living units is one of their prime characteristics; they do not merely aggregate— they form a collective. Yet such collectives frequently are reversible; they form or disband depending upon circumstances or preference. Reversible collectives may be called facultative. They are illustrated by a colony of bacteria, the properties of whose members are somewhat altered in the association but which can be dispersed at will to form individuals capable of forming new identical colonies. The defining conditions for a facultative collective are:

$$[nA]^R \neq nA \text{ but}$$
$$S \rightleftharpoons \text{non-S can occur.}$$

33

In contrast to this there are many living systems which exist as *obligate* collectives. Their components are very different in properties when in isolation or in the collective, and the collective, once formed, is not reversible. This is the case with most higher organisms and may be defined as follows:

$$[nA]^R \neq nA \text{ and}$$
$$S \neq \text{non-S}$$

There are, of course, many gradations between facultative and obligate collectives. A complex multicellular organism represents an extreme case in which very special conditions are required to maintain individual cells or individual organs outside of the collective relationship. What needs to be recognized and explained is the fact that living systems have tended toward higher levels of order of obligate type; they have produced ever more encompassing relationships of this kind. Each living set tends to produce subsets and to associate in higher order sets, and both tendencies repeat phylogenetically and ontogenetically. The history of organisms and the history of the whole biotic mass has been one of successive production of higher and higher orders of obligate collectives.

My focus here will be on the fact that obligate collectives reproduce themselves and that each generation of higher order obligate collectives turns back to a lower order of complexity for reproduction and then returns to higher order in developmental progression. I am going to concentrate attention largely on ontogenetic progression of complexity— on the increasing levels of order that occur in each successive generation of higher organisms. In this phenomenon we are forced to face the difficult questions of the derivation of

34

properties and behaviors at one level from those of another.

Let me repeat for emphasis that organisms deal with the problem of replication of higher levels of order by replicating information at relatively low levels of order and then successively translating and transforming this information to generate higher levels of order. Biological order, as we have noted, exists at a number of levels in the living world, but fundamentally it is replicated at molecular levels followed by re-establishment of higher orders through successive transformations of information into collectives at a higher level. Students of development squarely face the problem of translation of properties from one level of order to the next because it happens repeatedly in each new generation. In order to understand development we have to understand the rules of translation from lower to higher level.

This was realized, of course, many years ago. The early Greeks who first contemplated the phenomenon of development were amazed at the emergence of order that occurred in each generation. They tried fruitlessly to explain how this could occur. Over the centuries two general ways of coping with the problem appeared. One essentially defined away the problem by supposing that the total order is really present in miniature at the beginning of each generation and merely gets scaled up. The alternative to this preformationist view was the supposition that order is reformed *de novo* in each generation, the view referred to as epigenesis. In extreme form it posited repeated spontaneous generation without any continuity with the past. As you know, we are now thoroughly convinced that properties of successive generations are continuous, and that each generation begins with some amount of transmitted basic information which needs to be extensively processed before giving rise again to the maximum order of the fully formed adult.

Figure 2 is a simplified diagram to show the way in which the basic information or genome of the egg is replicated and translated to provide the ordered diversity which characterizes adult organisms. The genome is represented as a linear array since we know that the fundamental initiating information is contained in the mixed polymeric linear molecules known as DNA. The molecules of DNA are replicated in every successive division cycle of the cell, both within a single multicellular generation and to provide the linkage to succeeding generations. Each localized region of the genome (gene) produces a transcribed RNA message which directs the protein synthetic machinery in the cell-components known as ribosomes, where translation of the ordered se-

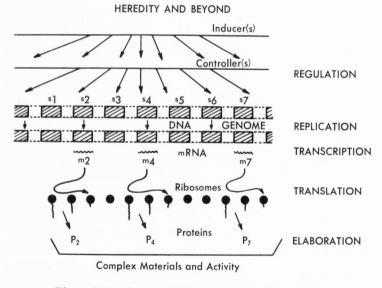

Figure 2. Replication and translation of the genome.

quence of nucleotide units of DNA to the ordered sequence of amino acid units of protein is completed. The proteins thus produced then either themselves directly become units in the structure and activity of the adult or they direct synthesis of further units which do so. Hence the diagram displays the role of replication (DNA to DNA), transcription (DNA to RNA), translation (RNA to protein) and elaboration of gene products into the complexity of the adult.

The word elaboration covers a wide gap—for example, from a linear order of amino acids to the three-dimensional (four-dimensional if one takes time into account) pattern of a human being. Are all the necessary properties for the final complexity contained in the linear order? If not, where are the others? To the extent that the linear order contains the properties, how do they get transformed to other and higher systems of order? Let us call the origin of new systems of order (higher order sets) neogenesis. It is my purpose to show that new properties arise or emerge in neogenesis, and that they do so in ways that we do not yet fully understand but which are not basically mysterious and are potentially comprehensible.

Neogenesis may be broken down into a series of steps that we may now examine in more detail. The first involves interactions among gene products by mechanisms which are similar and repetitive. Molecules of similar kind become associated with one another to form a multimolecular system, a set of higher order than the molecule; i.e., a macromolecular complex. Such interactions may be homologous, between like molecules, or they may be heterologous, between unlike molecules. The properties of the molecules which determine these interactions relate to amino-acid sequence, but not in a direct or simple way. The linear array of amino acids is first transformed by the folding of the molecule without any change of sequence. In this instance, how do the specific properties for interaction arise? It is clear that the new properties derive from changed relationships (R) among the amino acid components initially set in place by the inherited information.

The physical chemistry of a protein molecule provides excellent insight into the problems. The primary structure of proteins is established by the polypeptide backbone, with amino acid linked to amino acid via amino and carboxyl junction points. It is this structure which is the direct product of the inherited order. What is called secondary structure emerges from degrees of freedom at the junction points between amino acids, together with specific properties of the individual amino acids. The most probable secondary structure is stabilized by various secondary linkages between the amino acid side chains.

We are beginning to understand the way in which the basic polypeptide linear order of a protein is transformed into a three-dimensional configuration (Figure 3) (e.g., See Anfinsen). The steps are a function of the properties of the individual amino acids making up the chain. The way in which the folding occurs depends upon the amino acid sequence and particularly upon the strategic location of certain chemical groups of several kinds. For example, some of the amino acids along the chain have side groups which are hydrophilic and some hydrophobic. The general tendency in water solution is for the hydrophobic side groups, the ones not readily miscible with water, to move into the interior. The hydrophilic ones, on the other hand, tend to remain at the surface. The difference between the hydrophobic and

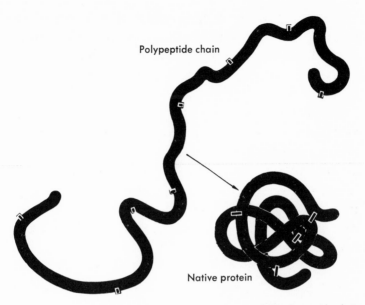

Schematic drawing showing the conversion of an extended polypeptide chain to a native protein. During this oxidative process, sulfhydryl groups are paired to form disulfide bonds, and amino acid residues, widely separated in a linear sense, are brought into spatial proximity to form an active center.

Figure 3. Folding of polypeptide chain to form a protein. (From Anfinsen, C. B. 1968. Developmental Biology, Supplement 2. 1-20.)

hydrophilic distribution along the chain is an initial generating force to the folding of the molecule.

Also important are groups which can interact and bind chemically. Sulfhydryl groups brought into close association are readily oxidized to form disulphide bonds and thus frequently act to stabilize structure. Therefore, the new conformation depends upon the amino acid sequence, upon side chains of polar and non-polar type, and upon the positions of potential binding groups such as sulfhydryl.

A molecule may fold in one fashion if it folds randomly; that is, if the chances are equal that any particular half-disulphide were to join with any other one. Figure 4 shows a molecule folded under such essentially random conditions. Figure 4 also shows the same molecule allowed subsequently to restabilize by exchanging disulphide groups until the optimum configuration is found in terms of thermodynamic considerations. Notice that in this "native configuration" a critical "new" property appears—an enzymatically active site has been formed which was not present previously. Note that the site consists of several local areas of the linear order which are widely separate in either the unfolded or the random configuration, but are brought together in the so-called native one. Neither the unfolded nor the randomly established molecule are enzymatically active because neither has the configuration yielding a charge distribution essential for the active state. The linear distribution of amino acids does

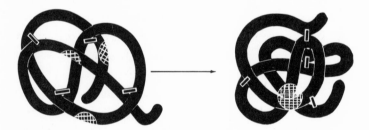

The spontaneous conversion of a randomly crosslinked protein derivative to the native form under conditions favoring disulfide interchange. Structural regions of the molecule that are involved in the active center are indicated by cross-hatching.

Figure 4. Random configuration and thermodynamically stable configuration of a protein molecule. Note that the cross-hatched enzyme region is complete only in the second configuration. (From Anfinsen, C. B. 1968. Developmental Biology, Supplement 2. 1-20.)

not by itself produce enzymatic activity—suitable folding is necessary for the activity to *arise*. Moreover, suitable folding depends, in part, on conditions in the surround. Beyond this, the resulting configuration only displays its special property when the macromolecule "happens to be" in the vicinity of some other system—in this instance, a suitable substrate. Note also that the properties that become important at the new, higher level of order do not relate equally to all of the amino acids but especially to certain of them in the new "surface" structure of the molecule. The enzymatic property is a derivative of the amino acid sequence, but it is a complex and selective derivative in which the properties of the surround play an essential role.

We can summarize by saying that the interactive properties of proteins (in this instance catalytic or enzymatic) are an expression of the relationships among the amino acids, initially linear but secondarily more complex. They are expressed in conformation, which is a transformation of the original linear sequence, sensitive to the context within which the molecule folds and functions. The initial relationships of the particular amino acid set established in one context are transformed in a new context. In the transformation to higher order a new property *emerges* as the *enzyme* is formed.

Let us look at another example involving not an enzyme but a structural molecule—collagen (Figure 5). Collagen isn't a single polypeptide. Rather several polypeptide strands make up the complex collagen unit molecule (monomer). Two of the three strands are alike and one is different. The polypeptide strands are one level of order, the three-stranded complex is a higher level of order, and the properties of this collagen monomer clearly are some derivative of the proper-

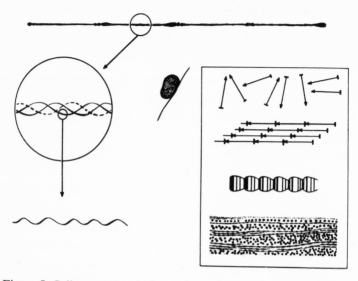

Figure 5. Collagen molecule (at top) consists of 3 polypeptide chains (left). Collagen molecule has polar properties and is aggregated into higher order architecture (box at right) up to a basement lamella. (From Gross, J., Lapiere, C. M., and Tanzer, M. L. 1963. In *21st Symposium of the society for the study of development and growth*, ed. M. Locke. pp. 175-202.)

ties of the three strands. Organization proceeds still further, however, in the formation of structural collagen which is the base for tissue architecture. Structural collagen fibers are in the form of highly ordered aggregates. Each monomer is different at the two ends; i.e., the molecule has polar properties. When the monomers associate, they may line up in parallel arrays, whose distribution is such that there is a displacement of a quarter molecular length in each neighboring monomer. This particular registry gives rise to a fiber with characteristic periodicity recognized as a banding pattern. In tissues, the banded fibers frequently occur not as individuals but as still higher order aggregates. Figure 5 shows collagen fibers as they might be assembled in a basement membrane or basement lamella. Here the collagen is interspersed with other kinds of materials which probably are also essential to the specific structure. Collagen, as part of tissue architecture, depends not only upon its own properties but upon the suitable interaction of collagen and noncollagen (e.g., see Gross, et al.).

Still further periodic structure of the collagen fiber, which is a new context-sensitive property at a higher level of order than amino acids, turns out to be consequential for still higher order properties at later developmental stages. Actually collagen monomers can assemble in a number of different ways (Figure 6) depending on the context. Among the possible structures, only the native periodic one nucleates the deposition of hydroxy apatite, an essential step in the formation of bone. Despite *the same information at the level of amino acid sequence,* only one form, dependent upon several contextually influenced steps, can participate in normal bone formation. Self-assembly from a genetically determined amino acid sequence can be relied on for continued development, but only in a successively altered and exquisitely regulated context. Each new essential property emerges from the amino acid sequence only in a suitably specified context.

This general principle can be illustrated at successively higher levels of biological order. Not only do relatively similar polypeptide molecules aggregate in specific order, but quite dissimilar ones do so as well. Thus, the proteins actin and myosin co-aggregate in a highly specific pattern necessary for contractility. In this fashion, contractile fibers and functional organelles arise within cells and these, in turn,

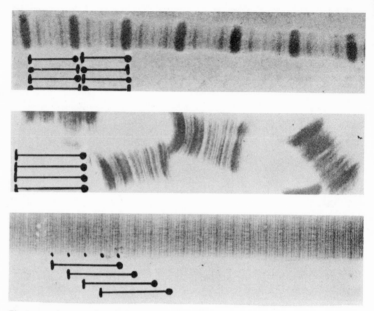

Electron micrographs of three forms in which a solution of collagen may be reconstituted. *Top:* Fibrous long spacing (FLS) with an axial period of about 3000 A. Molecules oriented at random to give a symmetric intraperiod fine structure. *Center:* Segment long spacing (SLS). Molecules oriented parallel and all facing in the same direction with no overlap. *Bottom:* Native type fibril with 640-A period. Molecules all facing in same direction but overlapping by about one-quarter their length.

Figure 6. Collagen fibers formed in solutions of differing ionic concentration; lower fiber in parallel polar array with one quarter length displacement. Note variations in middle and upper fibers. (From Gross, J., Lapiere, C. M., and Tanzer, M. L. 1963. In *21st Symposium of the society for the study of development and growth*, ed. M. Locke. pp. 175-202.)

give rise to such complex functions as locomotory behavior of whole organisms. In these processes whole cells enter into highly specific relationships involving both like and unlike types. Such associations of cells also involve a degree of self-assembly, but it must occur in an essential and specific context, and once again new properties emerge in the process.

The central point is that in each instance of neogenesis the properties that appear during the origin of the new set are not the simple sum of the properties of the components that make up the set. Whether the components are newly formed within the set, or are preformed and secondarily brought into association, the properties which characterize the set frequently depend upon a new relationship established within the set and upon the context, or superset, within which it functions. It is true that the properties of the new set are in some sense imminent in the properties of the components. Certainly these latter are *sine qua non* and in part determinate. Nonetheless, particularly in biological systems, it takes both a transformation and the establishment of a new context for these properties to be manifested. Stated in other terms, *the new information generated by the relationships that are established as the new set appears must be read in the context of the next higher order set.* Therefore, the emergence of new properties in hierarchical systems is closely linked to what we may call the set-superset transition. In both the developmental and in the functional sense, important new properties arise at the transition between a given set and its next higher order set. Conversely, such properties tend to be lost if components of a set are dispersed or if a set is dissociated from its context or superset. Properties of this sort can only be reconstituted if the components are reordered appropriately. The components may have enough information to reorder themselves, or they may require specific information in the environment to reorder appropriately. In living systems the latter is more frequently the case. In development, components of living systems form and order in a controlled environment that insures that their emergent properties will largely repeat those of the earlier generation. A nucleotide sequence or even an amino acid sequence is not alone sufficient to produce a new generation. The sequence must occur in an appropriate context which is largely provided by the initiatory stage of development. Here it is worth noting that DNA by itself does not either develop or evolve. It must be in the context of a number of other macromolecules to produce a living system, especially a developing one. It is true that something new constantly emerges in development, but it is also true that the emergence is largely predictable because it is repetitive of earlier generations. The possibility of non-repetition, however, is not excluded when context is sufficiently and perceptively altered.

In summary, hierarchical order is characteristic of living systems which tend steadily to enhance it. In the process new properties constantly appear, frequently under circumstances which suggest some mysterious emergence. In fact, emergence can be understood, at the sacrifice of all of the miracle but little of the fascination. Formal analysis shows that emergence relates to what may be called set-superset transitions. In these, determinate association of components provides new collective sets with relationally transformed information not resident in individual components. The new information frequently can be read only in a context or frame provided by another, often also newly formed, level of order. As an example, enzyme activity of proteins is an emergent property dependent upon amino acid sequence but manifested only after establishment of a specific configuration and in the presence of a suitable substrate. Hierarchical organization in biological systems thus is characterized by an exquisite array of delicately and intricately interlocked order, steadily increasing in level and complexity and thereby giving rise neogenetically to emergent properties.

REFERENCES

Anfinsen, C.B. 1968. *Developmental Biology, supplement 2.* 1–20.
Gross, J., Lapiere, C. M., and Tanzer, M. L. 1963. *21st Symposium of the Society for the Study of Development and Growth,* ed. M. Locke. pp. 175–202.

3

Hierarchical Control Programs in Biological Development

JAMES BONNER

BY development in the biological sense, we mean the series of events by which a fertilized egg divides and multiplies to make many cells, which ultimately turn into the right kinds of specialized cells in the right places at the right time to make the final, integrated adult organism. Development has been studied for a long time by developmental biologists and embryologists, but it is only really in the last ten years that we have begun to have some insight, on the level of molecular events, into what happens and what is responsible for bringing about the changes that result in developmental processes.

Before we discuss the developmental process itself, let us briefly review how the biologist views the cell today. It is the new insight into what makes a cell alive that has given us our new insight into developmental processes. We know that one reason a cell is alive is that it has in it a book of instructions which contain, in coded form, all of the information about how to make all of the molecules that are characteristic of that kind of cell. These basic molecules are the different kinds of enzyme molecules and the different kinds of non-protein molecules which are, in turn, synthesized by the chemical reactions which the enzyme molecules catalyze. The information-containing genetic material which encodes the recipes for making all of these enzyme molecules is, of course, the DNA of the hereditary material, the DNA of the genes and chromosomes. The chromosomes contain, coded in the four-letter language of the nucleic acids, the recipes for making all of the kinds of enzymes that are to be in that particular kind of cell. The DNA has two basic and important properties, so far as biologists are concerned. The first is that the DNA molecule can be replicated if it has access to the monomers out of which the polymer is constructed, along with the necessary replicating enzymes. The second property is that the DNA molecule also describes a read-out system of RNAs and enzymes which decodes and prints out the information contained in each gene in a form suitable for use in the construction of enzyme molecules.

Enzyme molecules are polymers, made of the 20 amino acids out of which all other proteins are made; and so to construct an enzyme molecule, putting these 20 units together in the right linear sequence, each 100 or more amino acids long, is an information-requiring task. The DNA supplies this information by means of the read-out system. A special enzyme, RNA polymerase, moves along the DNA molecule, transcribing the sequence of DNA monomers in DNA into an RNA molecule, which then carries the information contained in that particular stretch of DNA. Ordinarily the DNA is transcribed by the enzyme, RNA polymerase, in units of information about 1000 or 2000 monomeric units long, containing the information required to make one kind of enzyme molecule. The RNA molecules, each containing the information for making one kind of enzyme molecule, we refer to as messenger RNA molecules, since each contains the message for making one particular kind of enzyme. And although I am omitting many details of biochemistry, we do know that the messenger RNA molecule is in turn translated by a ribosome particle and other auxiliary enzyme equipment, which moves along the messenger RNA molecule, decoding the information contained therein and uses it to assemble the 20 different kinds of amino acids together into the right kind of enzyme molecule for that messenger RNA. The central lesson of molecular biology on the cellular level is that the DNA is a description of the parts of the cell, including the parts which read the description—the messenger RNA and other RNAs and enzymes, which in turn make the metabolic and structural proteins which take the food available and transform it into cellular building blocks. Some of these are building blocks for making more enzyme molecules and others are the building blocks for making more RNA, so that more messenger RNA molecules can be made, and thus more enzymes can be made. Finally, a portion of the enzyme molecules, of which there would characteristically be a few thousand different species in each cell, is responsible for transforming the food into the building blocks which make more DNA and help the DNA replicate itself, so that the entire cell can self-replicate.

Now, if we were looking at a single-cell organism in which all such cells were identical to one another, then we would now have a finished picture, because this description of the operation of the cell, worked out in the first instance for bacterial cells, is completely general. In a unicellular organism in which all cells are alike, all of the information in all of the genes is being used the same way, and we would have completely described life. Well, of course I am exaggerating about what we know. There are membranes and other complicated structures which are not yet understood. But even if we knew all about single cells, our picture of life would not nearly be finished because, in addition to independent unicellular organisms, we have integrated multicellular organisms which are composed of many different kinds of cells working together. Take us, for example. We are composed of about a trillion cells. These cells are very different in their shape, their composition, and in their function, as we can clearly see even without a microscope or chemical analysis. The central question of development is why they are different and how did a single fertilized cell generate such organized complexity.

All Cells Contain the Same DNA

The first fundamental fact is that in any given higher creature, plant or animal alike, no matter how complex, the amount of DNA in each cell of the body is the same. In addition, the information contained in the DNA of each body cell includes all of the information required to make the whole creature. That this is so has been known to plant science for a long time. We know of a good many cases, about three dozen by now, in which it is possible to cause a single differentiated and specialized cell—by one or another experimental trick (for example, making a wound near that cell)—to arouse renewed cell division and thence a whole new plant that is capable of carrying on through the whole plant life cycle anew. In the case of plants, then, it is clear that specialized cells do indeed have the entire complement of genetic information contained in them. Therefore, in plants development and differentiation into specialized cells was shown to involve no loss of a part of the DNA.

That the specialized cells of animals also contain the complete complement of genetic material of the organism has also become clear in recent years, particularly by work with Xenopus laevis, the South African clawed toad. The South African clawed toad was used for pregnancy tests in olden days, and therefore flourished in laboratories. In recent years, since there are other tests, the possibility arose that

Xenopus laevis would ultimately become extinct. Then, suddenly, John Gurdon, now of Oxford University, invented the experiment to be described (Scientific American, 1968) and Xenopus laevis has become again fashionable, and we are in some danger of a Xenopus population explosion.

John Gurdon's experiment consisted of removing the genetic material, the nucleus containing all the chromosomes, from a somatic cell of Xenopus—for example, a cell of the epithelial lining of the intestine. This nucleus he next squirted into the cytoplasm of an egg which he obtained from a female Xenopus. The nucleus of the egg was previously either scooped out or else just killed by a microbeam of ultraviolet light.

Now we have a Xenopus egg containing in it a nucleus of a somatic body cell, which, if it remained *in situ,* would never again replicate, but rather would produce messenger RNAs for making digestive enzymes and whatnot, and ultimately would slough off and be destroyed by autolysis. But when this nucleus is put into the egg cytoplasm, the DNA of the somatic nucleus starts to replicate itself and soon the pseudo-egg divides into two, and then into four cells, and goes through the normal embryonic development of Xenopus laevis, and grows into a tadpole, and ultimately into a normal, adult fertile toad, of genetic constitution identical to the donor of the somatic nucleus. So, it is likely that in animals, also, the total genetic information is contained in each specialized cell.

The Transcription of DNA is Hierarchically Controlled

These facts begin to tell us that the different specialized cells must differ from one another not in the stored content of genetic information but in the portion of the total genetic information that is actually used. We can verify this from other simple facts. We know, for example, that in humans we have two genes for making the two protein chains of hemoglobin. We know that those two genes are turned on for transcription of the messenger RNAs for making hemoglobin in certain body cells, those of the bone marrow, which give rise to the reticulocytes and thence to the erythrocytes. Also, we know that those same genes do not make the messenger RNA for making hemoglobin in other cells of the adult organism. Clearly the genes for making hemoglobin are turned on in one kind of cell and make their appropriate messenger RNA, but in other kinds of body cells they are turned off and do not make their messenger RNA. We can think of many cases which show that particular elements of the genetic material are turned on only in particular places. For example, the genes that make our hair grow are turned on on our head, and on a few other places on our body, and are turned off in such places as the throat. When we think of the developmental process in this light, we can at once sense that a good model would be one in which each kind of different specialized body cell uses only certain appropriate genes to produce messenger RNAs, and hence enzyme molecules appropriate to that particular kind of cell; and in which the genes which produce materials appropriate to other kinds of specialized cells are somehow repressed, turned off, kept from producing their messenger RNA.

Looked at in this light, the developmental process then becomes the study of the overall control of which genes are turned off and turned on at the right places and the right times to make the appropriate gene products appear in the specialized body cells, so as to assure that the organism will have the integrated form that we recognize as functional. Or to put it another way, the study of development consists of finding out what it is that determines the hierarchical programming which assures the proper, coordinated, sequential turning off and on of the right genes at the right place and time. This hierarchical program must, of course, be generated by the genetic material, because the form of an adult organism—that is, where the different kinds of specialized body cells are in the adult—is a hereditary characteristic. Things that are hereditary are generated by the genetic material in the DNA.

Switching Molecules Control DNA Transcription

We wish now, therefore, to talk in more detail about the developmental process from the standpoint of how the programming of gene activity is performed. What is the material basis of the regulation of gene activity in the cells of higher organisms? This matter is best studied with isolated genetic material in the test tube. It has turned out that it is very easy to remove chromosomes (interphase chromosomes, the chromatin) from cells of higher organisms, and in the test tube to transcribe it with RNA polymerase, thus generating messenger RNA from those genes which are turned on and hence available for transcription. Several groups of investigators have now found that the messenger RNA formed by transcribing isolated chromosomes in the test tube is in fact identical with the messenger RNA that is transcribed from the same chromosome in the living cell. So when we isolate chromatin, the stance of the genome—i.e., which genes are turned on and which genes are turned off—is identical, within the limits that we can detect, with the stance of the same genome in the intact organism.

The study of such isolated chromosomes has shown that in any particular kind of specialized cell, only a small portion of the DNA is available for transcription into messenger RNA. A large proportion is not available. RNA polymerase cannot get to it. In the chromatin of specialized cells with which we have worked, typically somewhere between 1 and 5 per cent of the DNA is turned on, available for transcription, and between 95 and 99 per cent of the DNA is turned off, not available for transcription. It is likely that the materials which complex with the DNA to make it unavailable for transcription are protein molecules; this is shown by the fact that the DNA of deproteinized chromosomes is fully transcribable by RNA polymerase.

Now a further point. We need to discuss for a moment the proteins of chromosomes. The proteins of chromosomes consist principally, but not entirely, of a class called the histones, which are found only in the chromosomes of higher organisms—that is, only in the chromosomes of creatures whose cells each have a nucleus. The histones, found only in association with DNA and on chromosomes, are characteristic chromosomal proteins which are lacking in cells of the more primitive organisms, such as bacteria and blue-green algae. The latter do not possess nuclei; rather their chromosomes are free to move around inside of the cell. Thus, it is very likely that the histone molecules, which complex to DNA in chromosomes, cause that DNA to be unavailable for transcription. They are, as the biologist says, repressor molecules.

During the last five years, my colleague Douglas Fambrough, now with the Carnegie Institution in Baltimore, and I have studied the chemistry of the histone molecules of chromosomes and have found that there are a limited number of kinds of them (Fambrough and Bonner, 1969): we distinguish eight kinds. These eight kinds differ from one another in their chemical properties, in their amino acid compositions, and so on. We have found the same eight homologous histone molecules in the chromosomes of creatures as different as humans, cows, rats, Tetrahymena (a protozoan), Neurospora (a fungus), peas, cowpeas, and frogs —all of the kinds of higher plants and animals that have been investigated. The chemical properties of the several chromosomal proteins of different species are similar.

During the past year, we, in collaboration with Professors Emil Smith and Robert DeLange of UCLA, have completed the amino acid sequencing—determination of the sequence of amino acids—in one particular species of histone molecule, histone IV, the histone easiest to isolate in pure form (DeLange et al., 1969). We have isolated this protein in pure form from chromosomes of cows and peas. We have found that this chromosomal protein, which contains 102 amino acids, possesses an essentially identical sequence in the chromosomes of peas and cows. There are but two conservative substitutions between them. Apparently, the gene for making histone IV was established long, long ago in evolution, at the time of the common ancestor of peas and cows. And the functions of this chromosomal repressor protein would appear to be so dependent upon amino acid sequence that evolution has been forbidden to alter it, although such alteration has occurred extensively with the amino acid sequences of all other types of enzyme molecules that have so far been studied. Apparently, a mutation in a histone molecule is not likely to survive.

The histone molecules are interesting, not only because they have the property of preventing RNA polymerase from reading the DNA molecule and thus making messenger RNA, but because they do not interfere with DNA replication. Thus DNA, when it is complexed with histone molecules, can be read by DNA polymerase, which replicates the DNA to make two DNA molecules from one. Histones effect a very special kind of repression, one only for RNA synthesis.

We have seen, then that the 95 to 99 percent of the genome which is turned off, inert, not able to support the making of messenger RNA in any particular kind of specialized cell, is complexed with histone molecules. But what controls which genes are turned off, and when? And how is a turned-off gene converted to the turned-on state in which it is transcribable by RNA polymerase? What is the nature of this hierarchical control? We know something about this matter, too, although there is still much more to learn. What we know about it comes from the study of small molecules, and by small molecules we mean molecules which contain a few tens of atoms only.

Messenger Molecules

Let us consider these small molecules. We know of certain small molecules which can enter a cell and cause genetic material previously turned off to become turned on. A good example in animals is that of the hormones, which are produced in particular cells of the body and travel to other organs. A hormone enters the cells of its target organ and does something which causes genes to convert from the turned-off to the turned-on state. Consider, for example, cortisone, which is made in the adrenal cortex and travels to the cells of the liver. When cortisone, which is a steroid, arrives in the liver, it behaves as though it were saying, "Liver, turn on the following series of genes, so that the enzymes which those genes describe can be made." These are enzymes that have to do with particular metabolic responsibilities of the liver, and these genes become turned on. And the same is true of many hormones, such as the estrogens, the androgens, the plant hormones auxin, kinetin, and giberellin. Thus, many hormones appear to effect their work by entering their target cells and turning on genes previously repressed.

The mode of action of the hormones is not direct. Suppose in the test tube we isolate some chromatin with its genes turned off and supply it with the appropriate hormone. Nothing happens. No genes get turned on. This is because the hormone, when it enters the cell, combines with a protein whose specific duty it is to bind to that kind of hormone and no other. This has been shown particularly clearly by my colleague Ann Matthysse. The complex of hormone and its hormone-binding protein then reacts with the genome, the chromatin. It finds the right genes, and interacts with the repressed DNA in such a way as to make the repressors fall off. We cannot yet specify how the hormone-complex causes repressors to fall off. This is a central subject in the white heat of research today. We do know something, however, about how protein molecules find the sequence of nucleotides in DNA with which they will interact. Protein molecules, in general, can recognize small molecules and bind them specifically. This is a general property of enzyme molecules which bind their substrates with great specificity. But, in general, while protein molecules can recognize one small molecule, they cannot read a sequence of nucleotides; i.e., they cannot read nucleic acid messages. We have found that chromosomes contain, in addition to DNA and protein molecules, also RNA of a special class. These are short RNA molecules which we call chromosomal RNA. Chromosomal RNA, bound on one end covalently to a protein, interacts on the other end with the DNA by base complementarity—that is, by interaction of A with T, and G with C—the rules of base complementarity discovered by Watson and Crick. These short RNA molecules, which are of the order of length of one-tenth to one-twentieth that of a gene, can read the DNA molecule by looking at it with the eyes of a nucleic acid, and determine what gene it is by complementarity rules. So we believe that the proteins find which gene to de-repress by using this adaptor molecule of chromosomal RNA, and that the molecule contains in coded form the addresses of the genes that it is supposed to go to and affect. We may mention, in passing, that in the cells of a higher organism, such as the pea plant, there are about a million different structural genes. These are genes which specify the sequences of amino acids in enzymes. There are, however, many fewer kinds of nucleotide sequences in the chromosomal RNA, of the order of 500 to 1000 times fewer different kinds of sequences in chromosomal RNA than in the structural genes. It would appear, then, that any particular kind of chromosomal RNA, which is on one hand responsive to some specific small molecule of the environment, must on the other hand simultaneously influence many different genes affecting the formation of many different kinds of enzyme molecules.

Development Programs Require Tests

We have now considered, in a preliminary way, the nature of the basic control event—the turning off and on of the genes—and the mechanism by which repressed genes get de-repressed. Now let us consider programming. When I first started to think about programming—i.e., turning on the right genes in the right places at the right times—I found it very difficult to do. And I still do. But I have found a good non-destructive way to approach the subject; namely, I just think carefully about how it could be done. Let us imagine that we are a cell, and that we are going to divide into two, and then into four, and subsequently to develop into something. What sort of control information would we need in order to perform this play? For example, let us imagine that we are the single cell at the growing apex of the bud of a particular class of plants that has only one apical cell. This divides into two and forms two new cells, the bottom of which starts dividing to make the bud get bigger, while the upper goes on being an apical cell. And in this class of plants, the cells in the bud multiply and multiply until the bud achieves the desired diameter. In the next step in the process, cells start turning into specialized cells; the ones on the outside start turning into epidermis, and the ones on the inside turn into wood. The ones that are in between turn into phloem and cambium.

Again, let us suppose that we are this apical cell. We divide into two—one is on top, and one is on the bottom. If we are to go any further along our developmental pathway, what must we know? We must know whether we are apical or not apical. Because if we are not apical, then we must go to that portion of the genetic book that tells us how to make buds. And if we are apical, we must return to the apical bud state, divide again in the right plane and make a further sub-apical cell which can turn into more bud, and so forth. Clearly, if we are a cell that is going to develop, we must have ways to *test the environment* about us and find out whether we are apical or not apical. How might such a test be performed? How could such a test be performed in such a way as to result in the turning on of new genes that were not turned on before? One way we might imagine that this happens is, for example, that certain genes produce (via messenger RNA and enzymes) a volatile substance. The apical cell, with its head against air on one side, will permit that volatile substance to leak out, and it will know that it is apical because it contains such a low concentration of this material. This low concentration of the volatile substance does not turn on the genes for making our cell grow into a bud. And when the cell is sub-apical, the volatile substance could, for example, accumulate and be the small molecule which, by interaction with its hormone-binding protein, goes to the genes that describe messengers to turn on the genes which are responsible for the initiation of the bud development pathway. This is the concept we refer to as the *developmental test*—the hierarchical concept that a growing cell in a developing organism is continuously performing tests of its environment. According to this concept, it is on the basis of the results of such tests that the appropriate genes are turned on to conduct the appropriate developmental processes. When we think of this testing concept, we see that it is a very general hierarchical control concept. There are many instances of it in nature. Take, for example, the case of the Xenopus egg mentioned above. A nucleus, the genetic material of an epithelial cell of the gut, which is producing messenger RNA for making digestive enzymes, also makes ribosomes, etcetera, but does not make enzymes for making more DNA. In the Gurdon experiment this genetic material is placed into a fertilized egg cytoplasm. The new genetic material looks out and it sees certain materials of the fertilized egg—whatever they are (and no one knows the responsible substances yet). They are small molecules which by their appropriate concentrations turn on the genes responsible for making a creature develop along the embryonic developmental pathway. We can observe the genes of the gut genome being reset; the genes for making ribosomes get turned off; the genes for making the enzymes that cause the DNA replication get turned on; and our cell starts off on the pathway dictated by the small molecules in the cytoplasm of the egg. A further example is even simpler and more illuminating. This is the example of the potato tuber. A potato tuber is covered with an epidermis. The tuber is also full of parenchymatous cells which are full of starch. We like these cells and eat them. As long as the potato is intact, the parenchymatous cells on the inside have their genetic material almost completely turned off; they are almost completely inert. They don't make any messenger RNA, and hence make no enzymes. But if a biologist cuts a slice out of the potato tuber, then over a period of a few hours the cells at the edges, which otherwise would not have ever divided again, all start to divide. They gather from their genome the information about how to make a new skin, and they try to make a new skin around the slice. The basis of this response is understood to a considerable degree. It has been shown by George Laties (1963) that the cells of the potato tuber continuously make a volatile substance which is either iso-amylalcohol or something very much like it. As long as the potato tuber is intact, this volatile substance cannot leak out and it builds up a required threshold concentration, at which all genes are turned off, or almost all genes —all except the ones that make the enzyme that produces that iso-amylalcohol. When we cut a slice out of the tuber the concentration of this volatile material at the surface of the slice goes to zero, or at least to a low level. It is the low level of the material which results in the turning on of the genes required for making cell division start again. And indeed, cell division in such slices can be inhibited by putting the slice in an atmosphere which contains the gas pumped out from the inside of a potato tuber or in an atmosphere which contains air to which has been added the appropriate amount of iso-amylalcohol. We can think of many further examples of this kind of cell control during development which looks as though the cell is determining its next step on the basis of tests for certain kinds of small molecules it finds around it.

Let us now return to the example of the apical bud and stem. The apical cell divides into two, and the sub-apical cell divides into four, and these divide into eight to make a still broader stem. How do the cells in the developing bud know when to stop making bud and transform themselves into the different kinds of specialized tissues? A good hypothesis would be that each cell in the mass of bud may have a way of measuring (again a chemical way) how big the mass of cells in which it is embedded is. And when the cell mass, as measured by the concentration of perhaps some volatile material, achieves a desired cell mass, then the program says, "Let's go to the next step and see what to do—let's test whether you are on the outside of the bud, in which case you are supposed to turn into epidermis."

Development Programs Require Hierarchical Levels

Five years ago I played with the idea of trying to simulate a developmental process by asking myself, for each step in the development of a plant organ, what kinds of information I would need to go on to the next. Four years ago two of my colleagues and I, including Douglas Brutlag, took a further step. We wrote a program in Fortran IV, describing in detail the step by step developmental process by which a single apical cell could give rise to the cell elements which, in turn, give rise to the differentiated tissues of the stem. When one writes a program in Fortran, or in any other language, one has to think in depth and with a precision and logic that is not used in everyday thought. We found that we were unable to write, or at least to readily write, a program for causing the development of a single cell into a complicated organism unless we added, in addition to the concept of the environmental test, another hierarchical concept. This is the concept we call *developmental pathway* or *phase*. For example, when the developing cell is in the stage of making bud, it is doing all the kinds of tests of environment which are appropriate to control what a cell should do while it is inside a bud. But those same tests are not appropriate if you are a cell in a root, or flower, or someplace else. And we found, in order to write our Fortran program in rigorous detail, it was required to insert the concept that cells in the bud make tests appropriate to the bud, but that when the bud is finished, the bud phase is over, and we turn off all the tests appropriate for bud-making and turn on instead a set of developmental tests appropriate for the development of the differentiated tissues of the stem. When we stop to think about this matter we see that that choice of test is a very general hierarchical concept too. For example, take cortisone again. The cortisone is made in the adrenal cortex and it goes to the liver and makes the liver do certain things, but there are other organs, such as the kidneys, and so on, which the cortisone also goes to, and in which nothing happens—certainly not as in liver. The same genes are in kidney and in other organs and tissues as in liver, but one organ is responsive to the small molecule affector substance, and other organs are not. The sensors which detect the presence and concentration of cortisone are turned on during one part of the developmental pathway— namely that for liver—while the same sensors are turned off and do not work in other organs that require other developmental pathways. The flowering hormone is another example. It is made in the leaves and it goes to the buds where it makes the buds turn into flowers. The same hormone goes down the stem to the roots, but it does not make them turn into flowers. The sensors that detect flower hormone and turn on the genes required to make flowers are turned on in buds, but turned off or absent in other organs.

And so we should think not only of the developmental tests by which each cell in the course of each developmental pathway controls the course of that pathway, but should think also of the control of the different pathways themselves. From the standpoint of hierarchical levels of control, we see in the developmental process that there is first the level of the determination of which pathway is to be followed —embryonic development or, later, pathways leading to head or eyes, or limbs, or liver. We do not know how many pathways there are. I sat down and tried to write them out for pea plants. I immediately wrote out about 30 different developmental pathways that must necessarily be involved in the development of a plant, and I presume that in the development of a higher animal, such as ourselves, there must be even more pathways. So we turn on the set of genes which generates this pathway. That is hierarchical level number 1, or the highest developmental control level.

The next lower hierarchical level, which results from the genes for a given pathway being turned on, are the genes which are responsible for turning on the genes that make the molecules that sense the concentration of particular kinds of molecules in the environment. The lowest level is made up of the final structural genes which contain the coded information for making the different kinds of enzyme molecules —for example, the genes which are turned on in response to the determination by the cortisone-sensing gene that there is an appropriate concentration of cortisone. There are, of course, other systems and levels of control, such as the control of activity on the level of the enzyme. However, we tend to consider this a different subject from that of development itself.

These are exciting days for the study of developmental processes. We do not know enough about developmental processes. We know little of their origins, and we do not know in molecular detail how the three principal hierarchical levels of control are integrated and inter-controlled, but we are beginning to understand how hierarchical controls function and why they are necessary for life.

REFERENCES

DeLange, R., Fambrough, D., Smith, E., and Bonner, J. 1969. Calf and pea histone IV. 3. Complete amino acid sequence of pea seedling histone IV; Comparison with the homologous calf thymus histone. *J. of Biol. Chem.* 244:5669.

Fambrough, D. and Bonner, J. 1969. Limited molecular heterogeneity of plant histones. *Biochimica et Biophysica Acta* 175:113

Gurdon, John. 1968. Transplanted nuclei and cell differentiation. *Scientific American,* Dec. 216:24

Laties, G. 1963. *Control Mechanisms in Respiration and Fermentation,* B. Wright, ed. Ronald Press, New York.

4

The Physical Basis and Origin of Hierarchical Control

H. H. PATTEE

MY study of hierarchical organization began from the point of view of a physicist interested in the origin of life. I would not choose to study a concept that is so general and so poorly defined, except that no matter how I have looked at the question of the origin of life, I have not been able to evade the problem of the origin of hierarchical control. Hierarchical organization is so universal in the biological world that we usually pass it off as the natural way to achieve simplicity or efficiency in a large collection of interacting elements. If asked what the fundamental reason is for hierarchical organization, I suspect most people would simply say, "How else would you do it?"

This existential response has the right hierarchical spirit, for indeed one central result of hierarchical organization is greater simplicity; and yet any analytical approach to understanding simplicity always turns out to be very complex. We do not really mean just "simplicity" but *functional* simplicity. The elegance of a physical theory or a work of art depends on simplicity, but never on simplicity alone. There must also be a measure of effectiveness. In the same way, the simplification that results from the hierarchical constraints of an organizaton must be balanced by how well it functions.

What are the central problems about hierarchical systems? First there is the apparent paradox that hierarchical controls both limit freedom and give more freedom at the same time. The constraints of the genetic code on ordinary chemistry make possible the diversity of living forms. At the next level, the additional constraints of genetic repressors make possible the integrated development of functional organs and multicellular individuals. At the highest levels of control we know that legal constraints are necessary to establish a free society, and constraints of spelling and syntax are prerequisites for free expression of thought.

A second problem about hierarchical constraints is that they always appear arbitrary to a large extent. As far as we can see, the same type of life could exist with a number of different genetic codes—that is, with different assignments of nucleic acid codons to amino acids. Molecules that perform the function of messengers, such as hormones or activator molecules, appear to have only arbitrary relation to what they control. Other hierarchical rules are more obviously conventions. We know we can drive on either the left or right side of the road as long as there is collective agreement, just as we know that we can give the same instructions in many different languages using different alphabets. In other words, hierarchical constraints or rules are embodied in structures that are to some extent "frozen accidents."

Even in the arts when there are no chemical or cultural constraints, the artist must invent his own. Igor Stravinsky writes in *Poetics of Music,* "The more constraints one imposes, the more one frees one's self of the chains that shackle the spirit . . ." and he goes on, ". . . the arbitrariness of the constraint serves only to obtain precision of execution."

In the inanimate world, there are certain types of constraints that produce structures that we recognize as atoms, molecules and crystals, and eventually mountains, planets and stars, but these constraints are not associated with new freedom in the collections, and even though some of the shapes of crystals and mountains appear arbitrary, these shapes could not be associated with any kind of effectiveness of function or precision of execution. This is in sharp contrast to all the hierarchical control levels of living matter, and for this reason any theory of hierarchical origins must explain the origin of the type of constraints that are both arbitrary and effective in the sense of giving freedom to the collection.

In contrast to the earlier chapters, it is going to be my strategy to approach these problems primarily from the point of view of physics rather than cellular or developmental biology, sociology, or ecology. At first this may appear as an unlikely strategy since hierarchical organization is foreign to most physics, but common to all the biological sciences. On the other hand, if we want to understand origins we must begin at a simple enough level so that hierarchical controls are not already inherent in the behavior of the system. We must ask what the first level is in the physical world where arbitrary constraints can produce a new kind of freedom of behavior.

Structural versus Control Constraints

What I am really asking for is the physical basis for the origin of life, which could be taken as the same problem as the origin of those control constraints that free living matter to evolve along innumerable pathways that non-living matter, following the same detailed laws of motion, cannot follow. In other words, although we recognize structural hierarchies in both living and non-living matter, it is the *control* hierarchy that is the distinguishing characteristic of life. Both structural and control hierarchies are partial orderings, like Simon's Chinese boxes, but the concept of control hierarchy is a narrower partial ordering that implies an active authority relation of the upper level over the elements of the lower levels. It is this original functional meaning I want to preserve, but without the original Divine implications.

Before trying to give a physical description of control, let me briefly review what we mean by a structural hierarchy. Simon, in Chapter 1 of this volume, has given an excellent description of the physical basis of structural hierarchies as well as a theory of their origin. His theory depends on the relative assembly times for elements with certain probabilities of association and dissociation. This time is drastically shortened if there exist stable substructures. Thus we find development of multicellular organisms based on single cells with high autonomous stability. In the same way, crystals are formed from stable atoms, and words are formed from stable alphabets.

The atom, the molecule, the crystal, and the solid can be distinguished as levels by the criterion of *number;* that is, each level is made up of a large collection of the units of the lower level. However, there is also a physical hierarchy of *forces* underlying these levels, the strongest forces being responsible for the smallest or lowest level structures. The strongest force holds together the nuclei of the atoms, and the weakest force, gravity, holds together the largest bodies of matter. There is also a hierarchy of dynamical *time* scales, which may be associated with the levels of forces, the shortest time with the strongest force and smallest structures, and the longest time with the weakest force and largest structures.

As a result of these graded levels of numbers, forces, and time scales, we can often write dynamical equations for only one level at a time using the approximations that one particle is typical or representative of the collection, that the fast motions one level down are averaged out, and that the slow motions one level up are constant. It is this type of approximate treatment of the dynamics of many hierarchical structures which Simon calls "near-decomposability." The simplicty and solvability of most physical equations depend on making these approximations. In structural hierarchies this interface can usually be ignored, except for the analysis of the errors of the single-level approximation.

Hierarchical control systems are not this simple. In a control hierarchy the upper level exerts a specific, dynamic constraint on the details of the motion at lower level, so that the fast dynamics of the lower level cannot simply be averaged out. The collection of subunits that forms the upper level in a structural hierarchy now also acts as a constraint on the motions of selected individual subunits. This amounts to a feedback path between levels. Therefore the physical behavior of a control hierarchy must take into account at least two levels at a time, and what is worse, the one-particle approximation fails because the constrained subunits are atypical.

For example, the development of multicellular organisms, which is discussed by Grobstein and Bonner in chapters 2 and 3, shows that the cells do not simply aggregate to form the individual, as atoms aggregate to form crystals. There are chemical messages from the collections of cells that constrain the detailed genetic expression of individual cells that make up the collection. Although each cell began as an autonomous, "typical" unit with its own rules of replication and growth, in the collection each cell finds additional selective rules imposed on it by the collection, which causes its differentiation. Of course, this is also the general nature of social control hierarchies. As isolated individuals we behave in

77

certain patterns, but when we live in a group we find that additional constraints are imposed on us as individuals by some "authority." It may appear that this constraining authority is just one ordinary individual of the group to whom we give a title, such as admiral, president, or policeman, but tracing the origin of this authority reveals that these are more accurately said to be group constraints that are executed by an individual holding an "office" established by a collective hierarchical organization.

In a similar way, developmental controls in cells may be executed by "ordinary" molecules to which we give titles, such as activator, repressor, or hormone, but the control value of these molecules is not an inherent chemical property; it is a complex relation established by a collective hierarchical organization requiring the whole organism. At the lower level of the gene, the authority relation of the hierarchy is often popularly expressed by referring to DNA as the "master molecule" of life, but here again we must emphasize that there is no intrinsic chemical property of DNA that allows it to hold this office. It is the integrated collection of "ordinary" molecules we call the cell that endows DNA with this authority. We should not expect that more detailed study of DNA, enzymes, and hormones would reveal other than ordinary molecules any more than we would expect that a detailed study of presidents would reveal other than ordinary men. The interesting problem of the origin of hierarchical control is to explain how such ordinary molecules and men can evolve such extraordinary authority as members of a collection. Or to put the problem in other words, how do structures that have only common physical properties as individuals achieve special functions in a collection? This statement of the problem shifts the emphasis from one level or another to the hierarchical *interface* between levels.

Rosen (1969) has expressed the problem in a very similar way by defining a hierarchical organization as a system that has more than one simultaneous activity (i.e., structure and function) such that alternative modes of description are an absolute necessity. As I shall show, this is also a characteristic of the physical concept of constraint.

The Structure-Function Problem

For many reasons, I wish I could evade this classical problem of the relation of physical structure to biological function. One reason is that it has generated so many polemics associated with reductionist, vitalist, and teleological arguments. A second reason is that it is currently out of favor as a biological problem. There is some reason for this. Almost all of the discoveries that make up what is called the molecular biological revolution of the last 20 years have been generated by a commitment to a strategy that says that to really understand biological function one must know the molecular details of structure. It was the persistent search for the underlying molecular structures in biochemistry and genetics that has produced our present descriptions of how cells function. Therefore, most biologists today hold strongly to the strategy of looking at the molecular structures for the answers to the question of "how it works."

Nevertheless, it is surprising and discouraging to find so many biologists who, finding this strategy productive, mistake it for a theory of life. Some biology departments have even gone so far as to exclude study of theories of life, as if the detailed facts of molecular biology had somehow demonstrated that theory is not relevant for biology. I was once asked by a leading molecular biologist, quite seriously, "If we can find all the facts, why do we need a theory?" This attitude is especially inappropriate now that molecular biologists are moving on to developmental biology and neurobiology where the integrated function is removed from the detailed structure by even more hierarchical control interfaces. One could not imagine a mathematician trying to understand the nature of computation in terms of how real computer components are designed and wired together. In fact, deep understanding of the nature of computation has come only from theories of computation, which are largely free of the details of real machines. As of now there is no corresponding theory through which we can understand the nature of life, but I shall argue that the study of hierarchical control will form the basis for such a theory.

Let me make it clear that I am not minimizing the importance of collecting the essential detailed biochemical facts of life any more than I would minimize the importance of knowing how to design real switching and memory devices that work with high speed and reliability in a computer. What I wish to emphasize is that the structure-function problem is still very much with us in biology, in spite of our new knowledge of molecular details. I shall try to show that this structure-function duality arises inevitably at a hierarchical control interface. We cannot understand this interface by looking only at structural details or at the functional organization. The problem is precisely at the interface between the detail of structure and the abstraction of function. In fact, what I shall conclude is that function or control can only arise through some selective loss of detail. The problem, which is especially acute for the physicist who believes that nature takes care of all her details, is to explain how a natural "selective loss of detail" can lead to hierarchical control instead of the usual loss of order in the system.

Remember, we are looking for a physical reason why an ordinary molecule can become the controlling factor in forming a chemical bond or in the expression of a whole developmental program. A control molecule is not a typical molecule even though it has a normal structure and follows normal laws. In the collection where it exerts some control it is not just a physical structure—it functions as a *message,* and therefore the significance of this message does not derive from its detailed structure but from the set of hierarchical constraints which we may compare with the integrated rules of a language. These rules do not lie in the structure of any element. We are asking for the physical basis of the hierarchical rules of the collection that turn these ordinary molecules into special messages. Or, to put it in the older terminology, we are still looking for the physical basis of the origin of function in collections of molecules. I prefer, however, to use the concept of hierarchical control rather than hierarchical function, since control implies the constraint or regulation of a total system, whereas function often applies to a specific process that is only a small part of the whole organism. I shall continue, then, by trying to say more clearly what control implies in elementary physical language.

What is a Control Device?

How are we to recognize the simplest examples of hierarchical control? How complex must a physical system be in order to exhibit control? Does control appear gradually, or is there a discrete threshold? To answer these questions we must specify more precisely what we mean by "control" in the context of biological origins and evolution. Let me begin to do this with some simple examples. First, consider an idealized process of crystal growth. Suppose you begin with a glass of water with common salt in solution. The sodium and chloride ions are free to move about in three dimensions. We say "free" only in the sense that they each follow the laws of motion of non-interacting particles with only occasional collisions with other molecules or ions. More precisely, we say that most of the time each particle has three translational degrees of freedom. Now suppose that after some time a collection of ions has formed a substantial crystal. This structure can now act as a constraint for some of the ions that land on one of its surfaces. These ions now have fewer degrees of freedom, like a ball constrained to the floor instead of moving through space. It is a collective constraint on individual elements that make up the collection. Do we mean, now, to speak of the crystal as a natural hierarchical control device?

I think not. My purpose in giving this example is to suggest that the concept of control involves a more active dynamical role than simply limiting the available space in which matter can move. The evolution of such time-independent constraints—that is, the addition of more such constraints in the course of time—can lead only to fixed structures, the crystalline solid being a good example. A more realistic variation of this example is the screw-dislocation crystal growth, which is a common process by which crystals actually grow. Instead of each ion binding only at the points of a perfect lattice, there are imperfections in growth which produce a new kind of constraint known as the screw-dislocation. This constraint has two properties: (1) It speeds up the binding of ions by an enormous factor, and (2) it preserves its screw structure as the crystal grows. This persistent speeding up of the rate of growth as the result of the collective structure of the screw dislocation is closer to an active control process.

However, the end result of adding such constraints is still a relatively rigid and permanent structure which clearly does not have the potential for evolution that we associate with living matter. There are many examples of the growth of non-living structures that have this final rigidity. The general difficulty is that we need to find how to add constraints without using up all the degrees of freedom. In other words, what we need for a useful control system is a set of constraints that holds between certain degrees of freedom, but that does not lead to completely rigid bodies. Of course, lack of rigidity is not sufficient; for example, a balloon constrains the gas inside it without freezing up into a rigid body, but a balloon does not have enough constraint on the motions of the gas molecules to be called a control device. A physicist would call the balloon a boundary condition.

What we need to find, then, is a clearer description of the degree of constraint that gives rise to a control hierarchy. We can state two conditions that must be satisfied. First, an effective control event cannot be simply a passive, spatial constraint, but must actively change the *rate* of one particular event, reaction, or trajectory relative to the unconstrained rates. This condition is fulfilled by most devices that we normally associate with existing control systems—for example, switches and catalysts. Second, the operation of the constraint must be *repeatable* without leading to the freezing up of the system. Another way to say this is that control constraints must limit the trajectories of the system in a regular way without a corresponding freezing out of its configurational degrees of freedom. In physical language this condition is satisfied by a *non-holonomic* or non-integrable constraint (e.g., Whittaker, 1936). Every interesting man-made control device must be represented as a non-holonomic constraint—switches, ratchets, escapements, and gear shifts being common examples. But at this point we must be very careful not to evade the problem by formalizing it. "Non-holonomic constraint" is acceptable jargon in physics, just as "derepressor" is acceptable jargon in biology. We may state clearly a mathematical function representing a constraint just as we may state clearly the function of a derepressor molecule. But such functions are not derived from what we call the fundamental laws; they are only added on as needed to describe the behavior of integrated systems. In physics the notion of constraint is not considered a fundamental property. It is not useful at the atomic or astronomical scale where the forces between "free" particles are sufficient to describe the motions. So even though we have another word to describe control, we have no idea of how control constraints actually originate. What we need to do is look more closely at the physical basis of natural constraints—how they can arise spontaneously and how they can be classified into structure-producing and control-producing relations.

What Is a Constraint?

The common language concept of a constraint is a forcible limitation of freedom. This general idea often applies also in mechanics, but as we emphasized in the beginning, control constraints must also create freedom in some sense. Also we must distinguish the forces that enter in the dynamical laws of the system and the forces of constraint. For example, there is the force of gravity and electric fields that enter into the equations of motion and determine how the system will move in the course of time. These fundamental forces do indeed "limit the freedom" of the particles, but the fact is that they leave the particles no freedom at all. Or to put it more precisely, the forces that enter the equations of motion determine the change in time of the state of the system as closely as determinism is allowed by physical theory. The whole concept of physical theory is based on the belief that the motions or states of matter are neither free nor chaotic, but governed by universal laws. So what meaning is there in our concept of additional "constraints" or additional "forceful limitations" on matter when theory says that no additional constraints are possible on the microscopic motions?

The answer is that the physicist's idea of constraint is not a microscopic concept. The forces of constraint to a physicist are unavoidably associated with a new hierarchical level of *description*. Whenever a physicist adds an equation of constraint to the equations of motion, he is really writing in two languages at the same time. The equation of motion language relates the detailed trajectory or state of the system to dynamical time, whereas the constraint language is not about the same type of system at all, but another situation in which

85

dynamical detail has been purposely ignored, and in which the equation of motion language would be useless. In other words, forces of constraint are not the detailed forces of individual particles, but forces from collections of particles or in some cases from single units averaged over time. In any case, some form of statistical averaging process has replaced the microscopic details. In physics, then, in order to describe a constraint, one must relinquish dynamical description of detail. A constraint requires an *alternative description.*

Now I do not mean to sound as if this is all clearly understood. On the contrary, even though physicists manage quite well to obtain answers for problems that involve dynamics of single particles constrained by statistical averages of collections of particles, it is fair to say that these two alternative languages, dynamics and statistics, have never been combined in an elegant way, although many profound attempts have been made to do so.[1] Furthmore, the problem has proven exceedingly obscure at the most fundamental level— namely, the interface between quantum dynamics and measurement statistics. This is known as the problem of quantum measurement, and although it has been discussed by the most competent physicists since quantum mechanics was discovered, it is still in an unsatisfactory state. What is agreed, however, is that measurement requires an *alternative description,* which is not derivable from quantum dynamical equa-

1. How well the dynamical and statistical descriptions have been combined is, of course, a matter of opinion. The basic problem is that the dynamical equations of matter are strictly reversible in time, whereas collections of matter approaching equilibrium are irreversible. The resolutions of this problem have been central to the development of statistical mechanics and have produced many profound arguments. For our purposes we need not judge the quality of these arguments, but only note that the resolutions always involve *alternative descriptions* of the same physical situation. (See e.g., Uhlenbeck and Ford, 1963)

tions of motion.[2] Bearing in mind that even the clearest physical picture of a constraint involves a hierarchical interface which needs more careful analysis, we may distinguish some of the more common types of structures that we observe to originate spontaneously. We are still looking for conditions that would favor control constraints, but we must begin with the better understood structural constraints.

The chemical bond is undoubtedly the most fundamental structure in the energy range where we recognize life processes. But is it useful to consider this structure as a constraint in the language of control systems? One could argue that since the structures of atoms and molecules are stationary states, they are in a definite state of precise energy, and therefore time is excluded by the uncertainty principle. Thus, we might say that to describe this as a constraint we relinquish the detailed time description of the motion. However, in this case, the structure is really a solution of the equations of motion, and the fact that the energy and time are not simultaneously measurable is not the result of collective forces or an averaging process, but an essential condition of the fundamental dynamical language of quantum mechanics. In other words, the laws determine the structures—there is

2. The quantum measurement problem is closely related to the statistical irreversibility problem, and it too has a long history of profound arguments central to the interpretation of quantum theory. The basic difficulty here is that a physical event, such as a collision of two particles, is a reversible process, whereas the record of this event, which we call a measurement, is irreversible (the record cannot precede the event). Yet, if we look at the recording device in detail, it should then be reducible to reversible collisions between collections of particles. Again for our discussion here it is not necessary to judge the many attempts to resolve this difficulty, since as a practical matter they all involve *alternative descriptions* for the event and the record of the event. (See, e.g., von Neumann, J., 1955, for a mathematical treatment, or Wigner, E., 1963, for a non-mathematical review of the problem. For a discussion of quantum measurement and biology, see Pattee, H. H., 1970).

no alternative. I would, therefore, prefer not to call a single chemical bond a constraint, although it is certainly a structure.

But clearly all constraints depend on chemical bonds. A billiard table is held together by such bonds, and it is called a constraint because the motions of all the atoms in the table can be averaged out to form relatively simple limits on the motion of the billiard balls. So the question arises: How many chemical bonds do we need before we can speak of a constraint? Of course there is no exact number, such as 10 or 10,000. I believe there is only a very pragmatic answer that one can give: I would say that *a dynamical collection is described as a constraint when there exist equations or rules in a simpler form that direct or control the motions of selected particles.* Of course the dynamical equations must still tell us *in principle* how the whole system will evolve in time, without involving the concept of constraint.

In any case, our conclusion is that an equation of constraint in physics in an *alternative description* of the microscopically complex and deterministic motions that gains in simplicity or utility by selectively *ignoring certain dynamical details.* In effect, the physicist has *classified or coded* the miscroscopic degrees of freedom into a smaller number of new variables. How he performs this classification is not predictable in any dynamical sense, since this depends on the choice of problem he wishes to solve and the degree of approximation he is willing to accept. At the same time, it is also true, as we have mentioned, that the structures of nature fall into "nearly-decomposable" levels that differ in the magnitudes of their forces, sizes, numbers, or time scales, so that the physicist's classifications for a given problem often appear obvious and "natural." But this is a long way from a truly spontaneous classification, which could occur without a highly evolved living system. This kind of classification or selective neglect of detail still requires an intelligent physicist with a problem to solve.

However, I wish to generalize this concept of constraint so that it would apply even before physicists existed. Let me say that a hierarchical constraint is established by a particular kind of new rule that represents not merely a structure but a *classification* of microscopic degrees of freedom of the lower level it controls. The classification may take many forms, which an intelligent observer might define as averages of microscopic variables, or as selection of a few sensitive degrees of freedom, or as a redefinition of the system. But in some sense, the appearance of a natural constraint implies an internal classification process that is selected on the basis of simplicity, utility, or *function* of this alternative description. Now we are ready to ask what types of constraints will lead to hierarchical control. Can we state some principles of hierarchical control?

The Principle of Classification of Details

By looking at the idea of control and constraint in physical language we have concluded that a hierarchical control level is established by a particular kind of constraint that represents not simply a structure but a classification of the details of the lower level. Before asking what a natural classification could be and how it may arise, I would like to show how this principle of hierarchical control applies generally. Is it reasonable to claim that the selective neglect of certain details is a universal property of hierarchical control systems? Let us consider some examples.

What about the hierarchical control of the developmental processes? Here the lowest level is the collection of self-replicating cells. Bonner found that to represent the developmental process by a program it was necessary to use the concept of the *developmental test*. According to this concept, the developing organism performs tests of the environment or surrounding cells, and the outcome of the tests is to turn off or on the genes appropriate for the developmental response. Now clearly such "tests" must classify interactions. First, there must be a selection of what is tested. For example, such tests would not measure the positions of all the amino acids in the environment—that would hardly be significant for the cell even if it were practical. Second, there must be a selection of what range of results of a test will trigger a control response. Thus, out of the innumerable detailed physical interactions of the cells and their surroundings, there is a classification into significant and insignificant interactions, which I would say amounts to selective neglect of details in favor of only a very limited number of crucial conditions. Goodwin and Cohen (1969) say it is as though every cell need only read a clock and a map, but it is the classification scheme that creates the right "clock" and right "map."

Grobstein's description of the process of folding in the protein molecule provides perhaps the most fundamental example of primitive hierarchical organization. This folding of the linear chain of amino acid residues creates a new property of the chain—the enzymatic function. At the lower level of chain construction, each amino acid is recognized by its transfer enzyme and RNA and placed in sequence under the control of the messenger RNA. Here there is no doubt that certain detailed structures identifying each amino acid must be crucial for accurate construction, whereas on the next level up, when we can use an alternative description of the amino acid collection appropriate to its *function* as an enzyme, such detail is no longer necessary. In fact, there is good experimental evidence that there are equivalence classes of amino acids in the chain which allow the same enzymatic function (e.g., see Nolan and Margoliash, 1969).

At the other extreme of complexity, in human organizations and political hierarchies, there are also many examples of the selective ignoring of details. Indeed, at no other level do the rules of classification and selection of what we ignore appear so crucial to the stability and quality of the collective society. It is significant that these human rules about what we ignore are often promulgated as Divine moral principles or at least self-evident conditions for freedom and justice. The principle of "equality under the law" is at the foundation of most legal forms of hierarchical control, and this is little more than an abbreviated statement that legal controls should apply, not to individuals, but to equivalence classes of individuals, where most details must be ignored. An extreme example is the law that says that anyone driving through a red traffic light will be fined. Think of the innumerable details that this control implicitly ignores! Some controls also state explicitly what details we shall ignore, such as laws against racial or religious discrimination.

However, social hierarchies show us that legal controls may either ignore too many details or too few. In the case of traffic control, it is well known that a simple, fixed "constraint" of a four-way stop sign is not as effective in moving traffic as the traffic light that operates according to certain inputs from sensors in the road. In this case, the sensitivity to more details of the motion of vehicles results in increased traffic flow. But it is also clear that a traffic light which took account of too much detail, such as the number of people in the car, could not effectively increase traffic flow. In the same sense, a law that simply requires executing all individuals who have killed another person ignores too many details to be acceptable to society. A few more details must be considered such as the age and mental health of the individual as well as the state of society (i.e., whether the society is "at war"). But again, too much detail would make the control ineffective. The optimum amount of control detail must depend on the desired function. Punishment for murder does not consider the type of weapon used, whereas punishment for robbery does.

The Principle of Optimum Loss of Detail

We have looked at hierarchical control now at several levels, from crystal growth up through cells to societies. At the extremely simple level of atoms and crystals we argued that the concept of control implied a selective rate control process performed by a collection on individual elements. The control event is repeatable for different elements without freezing up the collection. This type of rate control is accomplished by flexible (non-holonomic) constraints that can be neither too tight nor too loose. If they are too tight, we see more or less rigid bodies with no "function," whereas if they are too loose we see only "boundary conditions" that have no definite, repeatable effect on the elements of the collection.

At the other extreme level of complexity, in human social controls, we also observe that too much constraint on too many details leads to what we might call bureaucratic "freezing up" of the system, whereas too few constraints leads to ineffective function, and ultimately to anarchy. It is easy to imagine how similar difficulties would arise at the enzymatic, cellular, and developmental levels of control if the constraints, or classifications they represent, are either too detailed or too general. Function cannot arise in a strictly deterministic system or in a completely random system.

This situation strongly suggests a second hierarchical control principle. We shall see later that this principle is especially important for understanding hierarchical origins. The principle states that hierarchical control appears in collections of elements within which there is some optimum loss of the effects of detail. Many hierarchical *structures* will arise from the detailed dynamics of the elements, as in the formation of chemical bonds, but the optimum degree of constraint for hierarchical *control* is not determined by the detailed dynamics of the elements. The dynamics of control is determined by how these details are ignored. In other words, *hierarchical controls arise from a degree of internal constraint that forces the elements into a collective, simplified behavior that is independent of selected details of the dynamical behavior of its elements.* It is the combination of the *independence* of the constraints on the microscopic dynamics along with the *simplification* of the collective dynamics which creates what we recognize as integrated behavior or function. This optimum level of constraint cannot be specified precisely—that is one of our problems—but it falls between the extremes of strict determinism on the one hand and the chaos of "equiprobability of accessible states" on the other. It is significant that the concept of "freedom" has meaning only in behavior that falls between these same extremes, and this helps us understand how freedom can sometimes be generated by adding constraints and other times by removing constraints.

It follows that the origin of an *autonomous* hierarchical control requires that the independence from detail arises spontaneously from this detail. That is, the microscopic dynamics at the lower level must lead to structures with macroscopic dynamical behavior that is independent of microscopic initial conditions, at least over some finite range. What kind of system has this property?

The Principle of Statistical Closure

When we think of simple dynamical trajectories, such as a baseball thrown to first base or a free satellite coasting toward the moon, we know that success or failure depends crucially on the precision of the initial conditions—that is, the initial position and velocity of the projectile and the position and velocity of its target. This is not the kind of dynamical behavior that leads spontaneously to hierarchical control. At the other extreme, we are familiar with chemical reaction systems in which, no matter what the detailed initial conditions of each reactant molecule, the whole system reaches equilibrium in a very short time. This is not a dynamical but a statistical process, and the theory involved is sometimes characterized as a description of just those aspects of the system that do not depend on initial conditions. Again, we know that this pure statistical behavior does not lead to spontaneous hierarchical control. In dynamical systems, any error in initial conditions eventually leads to chaos, while in statistical systems only chaos in initial conditions leads to simple behavior. What we need for hierarchical control is something in between these extremes, or more precisely, a combination of both.[3]

We have seen that hierarchical controls arise from a collection of elements, but act on individuals of the collection. The spontaneous appearance of collective constraints must therefore be a statistical property of the collection, but its control behavior must act on the dynamics of individual elements. The collective constraint cannot be a dynamical process, since its effect would therefore depend strongly on the initial conditions of its components, which would in effect make it unrecognizable as a constraint. In other words, as we argued earlier, a constraint has no meaning if it cannot be expressed as a simpler alternative description affecting the detailed dynamics. Such an alternative description must have a statistical character, as we have seen, but at the same time this collective behavior of the constraint must harness the detailed dynamical motion of the elements making up the collection.

This harnessing of the lower level by the collective upper level is the essence of hierarchical control. It establishes the

3. Other types of statistical behavior in between the dynamical and equilibrium statistical systems show a certain degree of self-organization. In strongly non-equilibrium systems, when there is a steady energy flow or dissipation, there is the possibility of oscillations, cycles, and spatial patterns of flow or chemical reaction which could be called hierarchical control (See e.g., Burgers, 1963; Morowitz, 1968; Prigogine and Nicolis, 1971). However, this type of control constrains only statistical variables of the system and does not directly limit the dynamical variables of individual elements of the collection, as in the residue-by-residue ordering in proteins and the switching on or off of single genes in individual cells. (See Pattee, 1970, for further discussion of this difference.)

"authority" relation between levels within a closed system. It is common to have structural hierarchies beginning with elements and passing to collections of elements, on up through collections of collections, and so on, but such structural hierarchies are open-ended; they do not close back on their lower levels to establish the control-authority relations. (Of course we may also impose controls from outside, but then we are not talking about closed systems or spontaneous origins.) This necessity for the collective, statistical constraint to close back on the internal, detailed dynamics of the elements of the collection I shall call the *Principle of Statistical Closure*.

Now at this point, one might ask if "statistical closure" implies any more than our original definition of a hierarchical control system—namely, a set of collective constraints that in some way limits the detailed behavior of the elements that make up the collection. What I want to do by using this slightly obscure phrase instead of the longer definition is to emphasize what I interpret as the most fundamental aspect of hierarchical control. It is in the nature of a "juxtaposition of disparate categories," to use Koestler's condition for a creative act. Closure is a concept defined in abstract mathematics that is a kind of constraint on the type of rules by which elements of a set can be combined so that no new elements are created. By the use of the closure concept here, I mean a collection of element types that may combine or interact with each other individually in many ways, but that nevertheless persist as the *same* collection when looked at in detail over a long period of time. The mathematical concept of closure is a discrete concept that has nothing to do with the *rate* of combination of the elements in the set. That is, the mathematical idea of closure is entirely independent of

96

time. Similarly, mathematical closure does not involve the possibility of error in local combinations or the number of trials over an extended time interval.

What I mean by *statistical* closure, on the other hand, is a collection of elements that is established and that persists largely because of the *rates* of their combination. This in turn implies a *population dynamics* for the elements and therefore a real-time dependence. Furthermore, the rates of specific combinations of elements must be controlled by collections of the elements in the closed set.

Examples of Statistical Closure

Since this characterization of hierarchical control is somewhat abstract, I shall give some examples from different levels of biological organization to support the principle that collective statistical constraints do, in fact, establish a closure property on the elements of the hierarchical collection. Perhaps the best known hierarchical control process in biology is at the evolutionary level, where the elements are the individual organisms and the closed collection is the "breeding population." It is a well-known principle of evolution that natural selection does not operate deterministically on individuals, but statistically on the breeding population. The effect of natural selection, however, must be recorded in the hereditary memory of the individual organisms. Therefore, selection is a collective constraint that limits the detailed structure of the individual elements of the collection and establishes a statistically closed set, which we call the breeding population.

At the next lower level we know that the individual is made up of many cells. Here it is not so easy to see what aspects of the development of the multicellular organism are statistical, or even that any statistics are involved at all. Many developmental biologists have adopted the language of computer science to describe the developmental process, as does Bonner in Chapter 3 of this volume, and this might suggest that only deterministic rules are needed to establish the closed collection of cells that forms the individual. Now it may be possible to imagine a strictly discrete, deterministic automaton model of biological development, in which each cell locates its position in the collection of cells by a mechanical test on the fit or state of nearest-neighbor cells, and then turns off or on its appropriate genes according to its developmental program. No statistics would appear to be involved, at least in the formal description of such a model, since the fit or state of other cells might be formally treated as a discrete, mechanical property.

But apparently nature does not do it that way. The individual cell switches off or on or regulates much of its growth according to *concentrations* or *gradients* of concentrations of "message molecules," and this is fundamentally a *statistical* process. Wolpert's (1969) "positional information" is a field concept that requires number averages. Even if some genetic controls are effected by temporal patterns of activity, as in Goodwin's and Cohens's (1969) phase-shift model of development, the concept of *phase* must involve a number or time averaging, which again is a statistical rather than a "mechanical" process. Since we lack so much detailed knowledge of developmental programs, we cannot go much further with this example. However, from what we know already, the developmental process appears to require statistical constraints formed by a *collection* of cells which establishes a detailed control on the genetic expression of *individual* cells that make up the collection.

Looking now at the cell itself, we reach the most fundamental hierarchical control level, where a small number of monomer types combine to eventually produce a replicating collection. The closure property is obvious, but where are the essential statistical constraints in the cell? Here again, as in the models of development, we can construct self-replicating automata that do not appear to have any statistical process or behavior whatsoever. Even descriptions of self-replication in the language of molecular biology contain no words or concepts that are as obviously statistical as "concentration" or "gradient." Many biology texts presently describe the replication process as entirely deterministic, discrete, mechanical events at the molecular level. Accordingly, one could "design" a cell, using only *one* molecule of each essential nucleic acid and enzyme that would reproduce itself by the same general replication, transcription, translation, and synthesis scheme that is used for real cells, although a certain amount of inefficiency might result. So how can statistical processes arise when only one of each element is necessary?

The answer, I believe, is in the statistical nature of the remarkable molecular devices that make this "scheme" work —the enzymes. Without enzymes there would be no DNA replication, no transcription to RNA, no coding, and no synthesis. The enzymes control the *rate* of selected reactions, and rate control is not a dynamical, but a statistical concept. The reason we do not so easily see the statistical behavior is that selective rate control in enzymes is accomplished by time-averaging rather than number-averaging, which we use to define concentrations. The enzyme (or a more primitive macromolecule with selective catalytic function) is about the simplest, or at least the smallest, structure that fulfills the conditions for a constraint given in a previous section— namely, a complex dynamical system whose functional behavior requires an alternative description of a simpler form. We said this behavior in a hierarchical constraint results in the control of the detailed motions of selected degrees of freedom. This is precisely the nature of enzymes. At the functional level, we speak of the enzyme "recognizing" its substrate, which means that its many collisions with other molecules have no regular effect, and even many degrees of freedom of the substrate are ignored in the binding and catalytic steps. However, at the functional level the operation of the enzyme is specific and repeatable—the same enzyme molecule producing the same catalytic reaction over and over.

Therefore, although any microscopic dynamical description of the enzyme and substrate must follow the reversible laws of motion, at the functional level of description we say the enzyme recognizes the substrate, catalyzes a bond, and resets itself; and all three of these operations are inherently irreversible and hence statistical in some sense. Here both our empirical knowledge of enzymes as well as our ability to construct quantitative models of selective catalysts is weak, and much more thought and experiment will be needed to understand this fundamental type of constraint.

Even though enzyme function is a statistical constraint, it is not by itself an example of statistical closure, since a single enzyme could not selectively constrain all the elements—the amino acids—of which it is made up. In fact, the smallest collection we can now observe which has the statistical closure property is the cell, for in the cell, each monomer of the nucleic acids and proteins is specifically constrained in its reactions by one or more copolymers made from this same collection of monomers. But the cell is too complex to have come into existence spontaneously. *The general hierarchical origin problem is to find the simplest or most probable natural collection of elements which exhibits statistical closure.* At the origin of life, the elements were very likely some set of amino acids, nucleotides, or both. At higher levels, of course, the elements are increasingly complex, such as cells or individual organisms. But at each new level there must have been a minimum set of conditions to generate a new statistical closure.

The Origin Problem

No matter how closely we describe existing hierarchical organizations or how much we appreciate their efficacy, their origins present a new type of problem. First of all, it is difficult to find examples of incipient hierarchical control or observe the spontaneous growth of hierarchical control. Human social hierarchies can be studied historically, but the forces here are so complex and always involve so many intuitive or rational decisions of the human intellect, that any relation with primitive hierarchical origins is thoroughly obscured.

In the field of evolutionary biology we can find many experts who take a rather relaxed and optimistic view of the potential for self-replicating hereditary units to discover new and more effective hierarchical organization through blind mutation and natural selection. On the other hand, there have always been critics who do not find the theory of natural selection a satisfying or sufficient explanation for the *major* evolutionary innovations that have occurred, in particular the origin of new hierarchical control levels. Recently, a new wave of skepticism has appeared among some mathematicians who have tried to imitate or model evolutionary processes on large computers. These attempts include a great variety of problems and programs, which have names such as problem-solving, learning, self-organizing, adaptive, or evolutionary simulations.[4] Even though many of these programs have been extremely sophisticated and have performed well on certain types of life-like problems, their evolutionary potential has been non-existent or disappointing. Of course, these programs have built-in hierarchical structures, but in no case is it obvious that a new level of hierarchical control could ever evolve spontaneously through a blind search and selection process.

The many detailed discoveries of molecular biology have not been much help in clarifying origin problems either. In fact, in one sense, knowing the details has only intensified the problem. Following the ideas of Oparin and Haldane and the successful experiments on the spontaneous synthesis of amino acids and other essential pre-cellular molecules, the origin of life appeared at first as a natural and very likely

4. Most biological simulations on computers are aimed at understanding or improving our intellectual abilities; e.g., Feigenbaum, E.A. and Feldman, J., 1963. Several symposia on self-organizing systems, supported by the Office of Naval Research, have covered a wide area of these topics; e.g., Yovits, M.C. and Cameron, S., 1960; von Foerster, H. and Zopf, G.W. Jr., 1962; Yovits M.C., Jacobi, G.T., and Goldstein, G.D., 1962. Examples of more recent computer studies of evolution are Bremermann, H.J., 1967; Reed, J., Toombs, R., and Barricelli, N.A. 1967; Conrad, M. and Pattee, H.H., 1970. For a discussion of the theory of evolution between skeptical mathematicians and evolutionary biologists, see Moorhead, P.S. and Kaplan, M.M., 1967.

event. However, now that we know the intricacies of the genetic code and its associated structures, we are again faced with what appears to be an extremely fortuitous hierarchical organization with no obvious process for its spontaneous origin.

Two rather undeveloped theories have been proposed for the universality of the genetic code, and are therefore closely related to its origin. One, called the stereochemical theory, assumes a direct fit between the structure of the three nucleotides forming the codon and the structure of the corresponding amino acid. The other, called the frozen accident theory, assumes that any codon could have been adapted to any amino acid, but that the particular choice was accidental and remains fixed because any change would have been lethal (e.g., Woese, 1967; Crick, 1968; Orgel, 1968).

To my way of thinking, these two theories evade the central problem of the nature of the statistical closure property, which establishes the *coherence* of the code and hence its *descriptive* generality. In the first place, all forms of codes, rules, or descriptions, even the most abstract and symbolic, must have a definite structural basis just as *functions* of all types must have a structural basis. For example, no matter how many adaptor molecules were required between the codon and its amino acid, each adaptor would in some sense possess a structural fit with its neighbor. If this structural fit were only the result of an inherent chemistry of the copolymers involved, then it is by no means clear why any set of copolymers should recognize precisely the set of monomers of which the copolymers are composed. In other words, a stereochemical theory implies that a *structural* closure property is inherent in the physical properties of matter itself. The stereochemical theory is not consistent, then, with the apparent arbitrariness of other types of hierarchical constraints or *descriptions,* or with the idea of *statistical* closure, which depends on the stability or persistence of time-dependent, rate-control processes in populations of elements.

The frozen accident theory, on the other hand, does not conflict with the idea of arbitrariness in the coding rules, but it does not help us understand the statistical closure property either. It is easy to say that a code will be "frozen" when any change is lethal, but the problem arises in the preliminary stages before the coding constraints appear frozen. The establishment of statistical closure may in fact result in an apparent freezing of structures, although there must be earlier levels of freezing before the time the present complex code was established. What we still need to understand are the minimum conditions for the spontaneous appearance of statistical closure in a collection.

It could be that the study of biological organizations in more and more structural detail at all hierarchical levels will eventually suggest the secret of their origins. Certainly such studies are necessary, but I doubt that they will ever be sufficient for a full appreciation of hierarchical origins. The basic reason for my doubt is that detailed structure alone is never a unique basis for any function or description. As we have argued earlier, the concept of hierarchical constraint or function requires an alternative description or a classification of the dynamical details; and the effect or message value of any control molecule is not an inherent property of its structure, but a collective property of a coherent system of molecules. This coherent system allows what we call the alternative *description,* which constrains selected details at the lower structural level so as to establish *function* at the collective upper level. There is, of course, a structural basis for any description or classification rule as well as any functional behavior. When we say that the DNA molecule is a description of the cell or the organism, we imply that there are enzymes, RNAs, and ribosomes to read this description. But it is not the structural details of these molecules that is essential; it is the properties of the entire coordinated set of rate-controlling constraints that make sense of each detail. It is because of the coherence of the set that we can speak of a description, and it is because the meaning of the description is in collective function and not in individual elements that their individual structures remain to some degree arbitrary.

Summary and Conclusions

The physical basis of hierarchical control does not lie at any one level of physical theory. This means that we cannot understand the nature of biological hierarchies simply by a finer look at molecular structure, nor by solution of detailed equations of motion, nor by application of non-equilibrium statistical thermodynamics. While each of these physical disciplines is useful for describing a particular level of biological organization, hierarchical control operates between levels and is therefore a problem of the nature of the *interface* between levels.

We have characterized this interface by three concepts we call Principles of 1) Classification of Detail, 2) Optimum Constraint, and 3) Statistical Closure. We assume that at the lower level of any hierarchical organization there is a microscopic dynamics of the elements, described by laws of motion, and deterministic in character. In order to speak of imposing additional "controls" on a system which is already entirely determined in its detailed description, we must relinquish some of this detail and use an alternative description. This amounts to a classification of the microscopic degrees of freedom—our first principle. This classification must be embodied in or executed by what we call a constraint, in particular a flexible (non-holonomic) constraint, which does not simply freeze-out degrees of freedom, but imposes new functional relations between them. The enzyme molecule is our most elementary example of such a flexible constraint that classifies its complex, detailed collisions according to highly simplified functional rules.

We emphasize that the physical description of this type of constraint is necessarily of a *statistical* nature, even though the functional description may appear as a very simple rule. It is this interface between the deterministic laws of the elements and the statistical constraints of their collections for which we still do not have an adequate theory or formalism, and as one might expect, all higher levels of hierarchical control appear to evolve from this primeval level.

Nevertheless, we can recognize several other general properties of hierarchical control systems that hold at all levels. The selection of the classification rules or the degree and type of detail that is ignored in a hierarchical constraint depends on the effectiveness of the particular function that is thereby established. In particular, when the constraints are too numerous or tight, or when they are too scarce or loose, function cannot be maintained. This is our second principle of Optimum Constraint.

Finally, the general property of biological organizations is that they appear to have an indefinite capability to evolve new functions and new hierarchical levels of control while maintaining a relatively fixed set of elementary parts at each level. In other words, the variety of alternative descriptions and functions does not appear to be limited by the fixed set of structural elements that make up the constraints of the organization. We call this Statistical Closure.

A physical theory of the origin of hierarchical control levels would be a derivation of these principles from a combination of the existing fundamental laws, both dynamical and statistical. It would explain how complex collections of interacting elements spontaneously separate out persistent and coherent descriptions and functions under the constraints that relate them. The origin of life is the lowest level of this process where the genotypes (descriptions) and phenotypes (functions) are generated by the constraints of a genetic code. As yet such a physical theory does not exist.

REFERENCES

Bremermann, H.J. 1967. *Progress in Theoretical Biology 1.* New York: Academic Press.

Burgers, J. M. 1963. On the emergence of patterns of order. *Bull. Am. Math. Soc.* 69:1.

Conrad, M. and Pattee, H. H. 1970. Evolution experiments with an artificial ecosystem. *J. Theoret. Biol.* 28:393.

Crick, F. H. C. 1968. The origin of the genetic code. *J. Mol. Biol.* 38:367.

Feigenbaum, E. A. and Feldman, J., eds. 1963. *Computers and Thought.* New York: McGraw Hill.

Goodwin, B. C. and Cohen, N. H. 1969. A phase-shift model for spatial and temporal organization of developing systems. *J. Theoret. Biol.* 25:49.

Moorhead, P. S. and Kaplan, M. M. 1967. *Mathematical Challenges to the Neo-Darwinian Interpretation of Evolution.* Philadelphia: Wistar Inst. Press.

Morowitz, H. J. 1968. *Energy Flow in Biology.* New York: Academic Press.

Nolan, C. and Margoliash, E. 1969. Comparative aspects of primary structures of proteins. *Ann. Rev. Biochem.* 37:727.

Orgel, L. E. 1968. Evolution of the genetic apparatus. *J. Mol. Biol.* 38:381.

Pattee, H. H. 1970. Can life explain quantum mechanics? *Quantum Theory and Beyond,* T. Bastin, ed. Cambridge: Cambridge Univ. Press, p. 307.

Prigogine, I. and Nicolis, G. 1971. *Quart. Revs. Biophysics.* 4:107.

Reed, J., Toombs, R., and Barricelli, N. A. 1967. Simulation of biological evolution and machine learning. *J. Theoret. Biol.* 17:319.

Rosen, R. 1969. *Hierarchical Structures,* Whyte, L. L., Wilson, A. G., and Wilson, D., eds. American Elsevier, New York, p. 179.

Uhlenbeck, G. E. and Ford, G. W. 1963. *Lectures in Statistical Mechanics.* Chap. 1. Providence, Rhode Island: Am. Math. Soc.

von Foerster, H. and Zopf, G. W., Jr., eds. 1962. *Principles of Self Organization.* New York: Pergamon Press.

von Neumann, J. 1955. *The Mathematical Foundations of Quantum Mechanics.* Chap. 5. Princeton: Princeton Univ. Press.

Whittaker, E. T. 1936. *Analytical Dynamics.* 4th ed. Chap. VIII. New York: Dover.

Wigner, E. 1963. The problem of measurement. *Am. J. Phys.* 31:6.

Woese, C. R. 1967. *The Genetic Code.* New York: Harper and Row.

Wolpert, L. 1969. Positional information and the spatial pattern of cellular differentiation. *J. Theoret. Biol.* 25:1.

Yovits, M. C. and Cameron, S., eds. 1960. *Self-organizing Systems.* New York: Pergamon Press.

Yovits, M. C., Jacobi, G. T., and Goldstein, G. D., eds. 1962. *Self-organizing Systems 1962.* Washington, D.C.: Spartan Books.

5

The Limits of Complexity

RICHARD LEVINS

CONTEMPORARY evolutionary biology is emerging from the coming together of the formerly separate areas of population genetics, population ecology, biogeography, ethology, and adjacent fields, such as adaptive physiology and biometeorology. This fusion comes about for a number of reasons:

1. The recognition that evolutionary processes are often much faster than had been realized, making evolutionary time commensurate with biogeographic time and ecological or demographic time. Thus, several new species have arisen in historical times: The apple maggot fly *Rhagoletis pomonella* was derived from a species that feeds on hawthorn sometime between the introduction of the apple into the Hudson valley in the 17th century and its description as a pest in the middle of the 19th.

The estimation of the intensity of natural selection in plants (Bradshaw, 1965) and insects shows evolutionary forces are often an order of magnitude stronger than was assumed by the founders of population genetics. The observations of rapid adaptation to insecticides confirm the belief that when conditions change suddenly or when a species is introduced into a new community, the genetic makeup may change at a rate which is effectively instantaneous on the geological time scale used in traditional evolutionary thought. The studies of Wilson and Simberloff in the Florida keys (1969) and my own work in the Caribbean show that the fauna of a region is maintained by a high turn-over rate, with small islands being colonized rapidly and species being eliminated quickly. Thus, it is no longer possible to assume the biology of a species to be constant during its spread or competition with other species.

2. Problems of environmental management, pollution, pest control, and resource utilizat. 'have forced attention to the behavior of whole ecosystems over broad areas with conditions varying in time and space.

3. The polemics of the early 1960's established the legitimacy of organismic and population biology as domains distinct from, although linked with, cellular and molecular biology.

4. Finally, there is a growing interest in abstract properties of complex systems as such and the ways of studying them, as evidenced by volumes such as this one. This interest in complexity is interdisciplinary. It is derived from diverse sources, such as engineering, cybernetics, operations research, systems analysis, management and administration, economics, and the qualitative study of complexity in the older tradition of Hegel and Marx.

The units of evolutionary biology are themselves complex hierarchies, as Grobstein's and Bonner's chapters have outlined. Each organism is also responding in complicated ways to a pattern of environmental heterogeneity. A population is an array of individuals differing in their genes, age, and physiological condition. A species contains many such populations varying in time, distributed irregularly in space, yet coupled by migration. And each local population of a species is part of a complex community of species, bound directly by competitive, symbiotic, predator/prey and other interactions, and less directly by their effects on their common environment.

Elsasser (1966) has pointed out that such systems may be so complex as to be in principle unintelligible in any detailed sense. The number of pairwise interactions between components increases as the square of the number of components, the higher order interactions more rapidly. Thus, a system of 100 components, each of which can occur in 2 possible states, could have 2^{100} or 10^{30} different configurations. If all sorts of interactions are possible, we would have to examine 10^{30} specimens in order to describe the whole system as a function of its components. But there have been only some 10^{19} seconds since the origin of the universe.

Yet we have the curious fact that systems are intelligible, far more so than if they were totally interacting. This intelligibility is not surprising to the traditional empiricist view, according to which the world is assumed simple until proven otherwise. But from the perspective of the new holism, even relative simplicity and intelligibility is a derived condition which must be accounted for. Accounting for the intelligibility of complex systems is both an ontological problem and an epistemological one. We want to know both how an arbitrary complex system behaves, and how this affects our study of it.

Our argument in general terms is, first, that the dynamics of an arbitrary complex system will result in a simplified structuring of that complexity. Second, the systems we study in population biology are the products of a long evolutionary history, the small group of survivors from among a vast array of organisms that have disappeared; therefore, we can apply what we know about natural selection and mutation to restrict our models to the kinds of systems which would emerge from evolution. Finally, the dynamics and evolution of complex systems result in structures amenable to the techniques of study that are now being developed.

The general strategy for analyzing complex systems is through some decomposition into subsystems and their interactions. In engineering, where the parts are produced separately, retain their identity, and behave in the system the way they behaved outside it, the physical components themselves may be chosen as the "natural" subsystems. Even here this choice may be misleading, but applied to evolved systems it is often disastrous. At any rate, we cannot accept these common sense components as the best decomposition, nor can they be accepted as fixed in the context of evolution. Without getting deeply involved in particular systems, this warning must remain a general caveat, which we may ignore in certain cases.

If we have a decomposition of a system into interrelated subsystems, it can be represented as a graph, or network, in which each subsystem is a vertex and each arrow from one vertex to another is an effect or interaction.

A fundamental property, an essential feature of the system, is its connectivity. How many subsystems interact with a given subsystem and how strongly? Stuart Kauffman (1969) has investigated the behavior of a network of elements, each of which is either on or off, depending on the states of its inputs. Such a network will start from some arbitrary initial state (some elements on, some off) and change, until it settles down into some periodic behavior in which some elements are fixed permanently (on or off) while others form part of a cycle. Kauffman generated his network at random, specifying only the number of inputs per element, but not the particular connections. Then a boolean function was chosen at random to specify how the states of the inputs of each element determine its state. The most interesting result for our purposes is that with a high connectivity (many inputs per switch) the system goes into a very long cycle. For instance, if every element is connected to every other element in a network of n elements, the system could be in any one of 2^n states. In fact, it cycles through $2^{n/2}$ of these on the average. On the other hand, genetic nets with 2 inputs per switch behave in a much more useful way; the average cycle length is roughly $\sqrt{n}$, so that even for large networks the cycle passes through a limited set of states. The significance of this is that natural selection operates through the probability of survival of a system. But probabilities are only meaningful if the law of large numbers can be invoked; i.e., if there are enough repetitions. Further, selection requires heritability—a correlation between the properties of a genotype at different times. But if a system wanders among many states, there would not be repetition in a reasonable time and selection would not behave in a regular way. The low connectivity gives high repeatability, allowing such systems to be selected.

Kauffman intended his networks to represent the mutual regulation of genes. However, the model may represent other organizations. For instance, each element may stand for a logical proposition, and the boolean functions then become rules of inference.

The cyclic behavior of the network now is equivalent to logical contradiction in its circuitry. We suggest that spontaneous persistent activity in deterministic discrete systems is the equivalent of self-contradiction in the networks.

It is not necessary to limit ourselves to on-off switches. Let each x_i vary according to some differential equation

$$\frac{dx_i}{dt} = f_i (x_1, x_2, x_3 \ldots).$$

It is well known that the local stability of such a system in the neighborhood of an equilibrium point depends on the

115

matrix whose general element a_{ij} is $\dfrac{\partial f_i}{\partial x_i}$. If all the characteristic roots of the matrix are negative, the system is stable and returns asymptotically to equilibrium after displacement. If any characteristic root is positive, the system is unstable locally. And if there are complex roots, the system will oscillate, the oscillations damping if the real part is negative and increasing if the real part is positive. Clearly, the roots of the matrix depend on the numerical values of $\partial f_i/\partial x_j$ in the neighborhood of each equilibrium point, and since the characteristic equation of the matrix of order n is a polynomial of order n, there will be no general analytic solution for $n > 4$. However, without solving the equation, it is possible to interpret the matrix from the graph of the system. Such an interpretation has the advantage of applying to all equilibrium points, and allows us to reach conclusions about the global behavior of the system. For example, a stable oscillation follows a closed path around an unstable equilibrium point. Therefore, if there are no locally unstable equilibria there are no stable oscillations. A system which has no stable equilibria, but is nevertheless bounded, will be in permanent motion. It can also be shown that a system whose graph has no loops of length less than three is everywhere unstable.

But it is not even necessary to look at the whole graph at once. If variables have very different reaction rates a_{ij}, they tend to uncouple and behave independently. For instance, consider a two variable system with the matrix

$$\mathbf{M} = \begin{vmatrix} a_{11} & a_{12} \\ a_{21} & a_{22} \end{vmatrix}.$$

Its characteristic equation is

$$(a_{11}-\lambda)\ (a_{22}-\lambda)\ -\ a_{12}a_{21}\ =\ 0,\ \text{or}$$

$$\lambda^2\ -\ (a_{11}+a_{22})\ \lambda\ +\ a_{11}a_{22}\ -\ a_{12}a_{21}\ =\ 0.$$

The roots are, of course,

$$\lambda = \frac{1}{2}\left\{ a_{11} + a_{22} \pm \sqrt{(a_{11}+a_{22})^2 - 4(a_{11}a_{22}-a_{12}a_{21})}\right\}.$$

This may be rewritten

$$\lambda = \frac{1}{2}\left\{ a_{11} + a_{22} \pm (a_{11} - a_{22})\left[1 + \frac{4a_{12}a_{21}}{(a_{11}-a_{22})^2}\right]^{\frac{1}{2}}\right\}$$

Expanding the term in square brackets we see that

$$\lambda = a_{11} + \frac{2a_{12}a_{21}}{a_{11}-a_{22}} + \text{terms of order } \frac{[a_{12}a_{21}]^2}{(a_{11}-a_{22})^3}$$

and greater, and

$$\lambda = a_{22} - \frac{2a_{12}a_{21}}{a_{11}-a_{22}} + \text{terms of order at least } \frac{[a_{12}a_{21}]^2}{(a_{11}-a_{22})^3}$$

Thus if $|a_{11}-a_{22}|$ is large compared to the coupling term $a_{12}a_{21}$, the characteristic roots are roughly the diagonal terms a_{ii}, which they would be exactly if the variables were all independent.

The same principle applies to subsystems as to individual variables: If the reaction rates within subsystems differ greatly compared to their couplings, the larger characteristic roots, which describe the short term behavior, will be nearly independent for the subsystems. This does not make the systems themselves independent—they affect each other as parameters rather than as covariables.

In a system thrown together at random, with reaction rates drawn from some distribution, subsystems can be isolated which have one range of commensurate reaction rates, and smaller subsystems may be isolated which have a different range of commensurate reaction rates and short loop couplings.

If we specify the kinds of components and the ways they interact, we can also see what happens as components are added. For example, let the variables be the population sizes of different species in a community. If these are all competitors, all the a_{ij} of the matrix are negative. Suppose, first, that species of the same kind are being added (that is, with the same average a_{ij}). The system will only be stable if the characteristic roots are all negative. But it can be shown that as the size of the matrix increases, this condition can no longer be satisfied. For a given closeness of relations (interaction coefficients drawn from a given distribution), there is an upper limit to the number of species that can coexist.

A more interesting model locates each species in some abstract niche of space such that the interaction between species or the probability of interaction decreases with distance between the species. Now the addition of new species means taking into consideration a wider range of organisms.

The behavior of this system depends on the way in which a_{ij} decreases with distance and the geometry of the space. In a Euclidean space of dimension k there are $c_1 c_2 r^{k-1}$ other species at distance k, where c_2 depends on the geometry and

c_1 is a measure of how tightly the species are packed.

Case I: $\int r^{k-1} a(r) dr$ converges. Then we can show the following from a consideration of the local stability properties of the system's matrix:

1.   There is an upper limit either to r, the radius of the system, or to c_1, the density of species in the environment space. In particular, there cannot be a continuum of organic forms—species are real.

2.   There is always some radius r_1 such that any desired fraction of the total interactions involving a species comes from within radius r_1.

3.   Maximum stability is attained by spreading the species uniformly over short distances but in clusters over greater distances.

Case II: $\int r^{k-1} a(r) dr$ diverges. Then there is no radius r_1 such that most interactions come from within that radius. But if most interactions come from a long distance, nearby points are subject to almost identical influences. The system behaves as a field, and the epistemology is simplified by the disappearance of individual components.

Although we talked of the components as species, the model has other realizations. For instance, I think it can be extended to describe systems of similar molecules.

There are two kinds of evolutionary constraints on complexity: Those imposed by optimality considerations and those imposed by the limitations of the genetic system. Fisher's fundamental theorem of natural selection states that selection increases fitness at a rate proportional to the additive genetic variance of fitness. Further work has revealed ambiguities in the meaning of fitness and has shown limitations on the theorem. But we can still make the weaker claim that populations in nature will generally differ in the same direction as their optima. This allows us to find optimal systems and use them as rough evolutionary predictors.

It is a commonplace in genetics that most significant "traits" are controlled by more than one gene and that most genes affect more than one "trait." This might be extrapolated to the situation where all genes affect all traits. A similar view at the phenotypic level recognizes that traits which are close to what we mean by fitness (viability under given conditions, reproductive rate, propensity to mate, etcetera) are themselves the consequences of a much larger array of "simpler" traits, which may be defined more precisely, but which are themselves of more obscure significance. Once again we could confront the totally connected system.

We will now argue that such a system will evolve away from total connectivity.

Let x_i be a large array of "traits" which can be expressed quantitatively, each of which affects all of a smaller array of fitness components w_j. If we specify all x_i except one of them, say x_1, then each w_j is a function of x_1, which has some maximum value at x_{1j} and decreases with the deviation of x_1 from that maximum. In Figure 1 we show fitness components w_j as functions of x_1. The curves can be described by many parameters. But we are interested in only two properties of $w_j(x_1)$—the location of the peak x_{1j} and the rate at which w_j falls as x_1 deviates from x_{1j}.

Fitness at one level is an array of functions w_j. At the next higher level, it is a function of these functions. For instance, if w_1 is the ability to catch and eat small insects and w_2 is the ability to catch and eat large ones, total food intake will be $aw_1 + bw_2$. But if w_1 is the ability to get enough food and w_2 is the ability to avoid predators, the survival probability

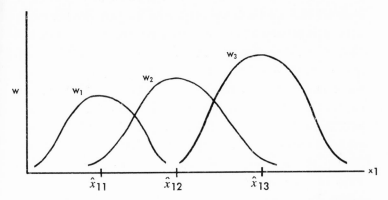

Figure 1. Fitness components, w_j, as a function of $\hat{x}_1$. The optima, $\hat{x}_{1j}$, are shown for each fitness component.

is $w_1 w_2$. In any case, the higher level fitness will be called the Adaptive Function $A(w_1, w_2)$. It is a non-negative, monotone, non-decreasing function of its arguments. The maximization of $A(w_1, w_2)$ gives us the optimum values for the underlying traits x_i. For this we use the fitness set method (Levins, 1962) in which the fitness relations of Figure 1 are shown in another form, as in Figure 2. In Figure 2 the axes are the fitness functions w_j, here limited to w_1 and w_2 for convenience. Each value of x_1 specifies both a value of w_1 and of w_2, and hence determines a point of Figure 2. The set of all points of Figure 2 corresponding to values of x_1 in Figure 1 is the fitness set.

The optimum x_1 is that value which corresponds to the point on the fitness set for which $A(w_1, w_2)$ is maximized. If the fitness set is convex, the optimum will correspond to some point on the upper right hand boundary of the fitness set which is neither the maximum for w_1 nor for w_2. The fitness set will be convex if the optima for the two fitness

121

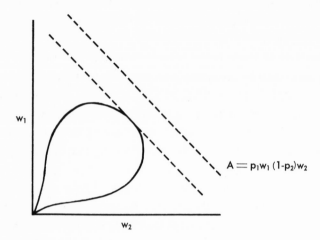

Figure 2. The fitness set for components 1 and 2 as determined by the trait X_1. A is a linear adaptive function which is maximized.

components w_1 and w_2 are sufficiently close together compared to the rate at which fitness falls with deviation from the optimum, and concave if w_1 and w_2 are relatively far apart. Thus, the first conclusion is that fitness components which are sufficiently similar can be averaged and treated as one, and the underlying variables x_i will have optima that are intermediate between the optima of the components taken separately.

If the optima for different fitness components are different enough, the fitness set will be concave. Then mixed strategies give fitness points lying outside the original fitness set. The optimization procedures are shown in Figures 2 and 3.

If the adaptive function $A(w_1, w_2)$ is linear, say $pw_1 + (1-p)w_2$, the optimum value of x_1 is the value optimal for w_1 if $p > \frac{1}{2}$ or w_2 if $p < \frac{1}{2}$. That is, the evolution of x_1 will depend only on one of the fitness components. If the relative weights assigned to the two components change so that p decreases from above to below ½ then x_1 is released from determination by w_1 and evolves in relation to w_2. Thus, instead of all traits being subject to all kinds of fitness criteria, traits will be clustered into sets each of which evolves as a unit under the control of one or several similar fitness components. But what we call a fitness component in relation to the traits x_i may be itself a "trait" acting on a higher level fitness component. For instance, the x_i may be chemical components of an insect cuticle; w_1 and w_2 may be heat resistance and desiccation resistance. These are "traits" affecting viability. Viability, fertility, and development rate are "traits" contributing to overall individual fitness. Population fitness is on another level again.

Thus, natural selection results in a hierarchical structuring of clusters of traits by adaptive significance. At any level, traits within the same cluster interact strongly, but different clusters interact only loosely.

If $A(w_1,w_2)$ is multiplicative, $A(w_1,w_2) = w_1^p w_2^{1-p}$ the situation is as shown in Figure 3. The optimum will then be a mixed strategy which must now be interpreted. A mixed strategy, in which a variable is not the same in all individuals, all parts of individuals, or at all times, has a fitness point on the straight line joining the fitness points of the components.

Suppose that x_1 is the pH of a cell, and that w_1 and w_2 are reaction rates for two different reactions. If the pH optima are similar for the two reactions the combined optimum is intermediate. But if they are different enough, a mixed strategy is preferable with the pH different in different parts of the cell or at different times. Once there is a heterogeneity of pH, this creates a new adaptive problem—the optimum enzyme structure for each pH may result in a mixed strategy

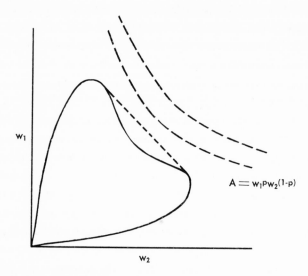

Figure 3. A concave fitness set for components 1 and 2. The dotted line shows the mixed strategies. A is a multiplicative adaptive function which is maximized.

of enzyme types. Thus, the organism's heterogeneity builds up.

The mixed strategy can be looked at also as the subdivision of a single trait, say pH, into two—pH in the cytoplasm and pH in the nucleus, or LDH into heart LDH and liver LDH. This is more obvious in morphology, where the optimum tooth shape in reptiles becomes a mixed strategy in mammals; i.e., incisors, premolars, or in the limb differentiation of crustaceans.

Thus, natural selection generates a double hierarchical structure. On the one hand, traits of diverse genetic control and physical form are clustered by adaptive significance. On the other, traits of diverse adaptive significance are grouped by common origin and possibly genetic basis. The evolution of an arbitrary complex organism is in the direction of the merging of some traits, the differentiation of others, and hence the emergence of semiautonomous subsystems in a hierarchical array.

The special rules affecting the genetic system also impose restrictions on the effective complexity of control. First, suppose that a given character is controlled additively by a large number of unlimited genetic loci. Then selection acts independently on each locus. As the number of loci increases, the intensity of selection per locus must decrease. But when the intensity falls below a level determined by the population size, the distribution of gene frequencies concentrates near 0 and/or 1. Most loci are near fixation. On the other hand, the response to selection is proportional to $sp(1-p)$ where p is the gene frequency. Thus, most of the response to selection at any time comes from the few random loci with frequencies near .5. The experimenter may report that such a trait is controlled by one or two genes on a particular chromosome. Different experimenters will attribute the control to different genes; so the complexity of control will appear as a heterogeneity of simple controls.

This model serves as a base for modification in two directions: non-linear fitness interactions among loci, and linkage. The former can best be understood through Sewall Wright's adaptive landscape model in which n coordinates represent gene frequencies and the $(n + 1)$st is some fitness measure. The stronger the non-additive higher interactions among loci, the rougher the landscape, the more broken by ridges, valleys, and saddles. A population is represented by a point which is moving under selection in an uphill direction and buffeted by chance in all directions. The greater the number of distinct genotypes, the greater the population size must be in order to reduce random drift. But since the number of possible genotypes is 3^n, if each of n loci has two alleles, most genotypes will be represented by very few individuals and drift will be important even in large populations. The drift displaces the gene frequencies from their pathway under selection, and much of the response to selection is spent keeping on the ascending ridges rather than moving along them. As the number of dimensions increases, the difficulty of optimization rises rapidly and after about 10 loci the rate of response would be too slow to reach optima within time scales over which the landscape is reasonably constant or the species persists. Thus, fitness traits controlled by too many high order interactions among genes could not adapt to changing conditions.

The role of linkage has been explored by Lewontin (1964) and his collaborators. The major striking result is that as the number of loci increases, the linkage disequilibria become more important, even weak individual effects of loci result in strong block effects, and the loci lose their individuality. As in the model of species in a community, very strong interactions which do not vanish over short distances convert a discrete model into a continuum. This is, of course, an epistemological rather than an ontological transformation. But it produces a new kind of simplicity from a system of initially complex strong interactions.

Now we can return to the original problem of the intelligibility of hierarchical systems. It is not necessary to postulate some unique rule for the synthesis of such systems. We do not, in fact, have to visualize these systems as built up from components, adding them one at a time, moving from simple to complex. Rather the starting point can be arbitrary complexity. The dynamics of the system itself and the action of

126

evolutionary forces on populations of such systems produces structure, merges some subsystems, subdivides others, reduces total connectivity among parts, gives spontaneous activity, and organizes hierarchy. "Confusion evolves into order spontaneously. What God really said was, 'Let there be chaos.' "*

REFERENCES

Bradshaw, A. D., McNeilly, T. S., and Gregory, R. P. 1965. Industrialization, evolution and the development of heavy metal tolerance in plants. Brit. Ecol. Soc. Symp. 5:327–343.

Elsasser, Walter M. 1966. *Atom and Organism.* Princeton: Princeton University Press.

Franklin, I. and Lewontin, R. C. *Is the Genome Made of Genes.* (in press)

Kauffman, S. A. 1969. Metabolic stability and epigenesis in randomly constructed genetic nets. *J. Theoret. Biol.* 22:437–467.

Levins, R. 1962. Theory of fitness in a heterogeneous environment. I. The fitness set and adaptive function. *Am. Naturalist* 96:361–378.

Lewontin, R.C. 1964. The interaction of selection and linkage. I. General considerations: heterotic models. *Genetics 49,* 49–67.

Wilson, E. O. and Simberloff, D. S. 1969. Experimental zoogeography of islands. Defaunation and monitoring techniques. *Ecology* 50:267–278.

*Rosario M. Levins: personal communication.

Postscript

Unsolved Problems and Potential Applications of Hierarchy Theory

H. H. PATTEE

I s it possible to have a simple theory of very complex, evolving systems? Can we hope to find common, essential properties of hierarchical organizations that we can usefully apply to the design and management of our growing biological, social, and technological organizations? Such a theory will require a deep and general understanding of the nature of hierarchies, how they originate, how they evolve, how the levels interact, and how failure occurs. The five authors of the previous chapters have explored the nature of hierarchical organization of complex systems from entirely different perspectives. As mentioned in the Preface, these chapters were developed from a series of public lectures that were scheduled over a period of months, so that the authors did not have the strong interactions that normally occur at conferences. Nevertheless, there is a common theme that runs through all the authors' discussions, and partly because of their independent approaches we may hope this theme has a general significance for a theory of hierarchies. One purpose of this postscript is to elaborate this theme. Again, because of the different perspectives of the authors, this has required a certain amount of restatement and interpretation which is my own doing and for which the authors can not be held responsible.

A second purpose of this postscript is to suggest directions we may expect the development and applications of hierarchy theory to take. Some of the difficulties are implicit in the previous discussions, but the selection of key problems is also bound to be a matter of individual interpretation. My own selection of unsolved problems is based on the aim of finding new methods for the design and management of very complex systems, since this was the aim that led the sponsors to organize these lectures.

This problem leads to an apparent paradox of any theory of organization. To "manage" any system implies adding at least one hierarchical level—the management level—which oversees the entire system. For this reason, there can never be any closed theory of hierarchies like a dynamical theory in physics. Hierarchy theory must be more like theories of language or programming that give us useful rules or methods for the most effective design and control of open-ended systems that can continaully grow and evolve new levels.

Common Properties of Hierarchies

The most common and most concrete concept we associate with hierarchical organization is the concept of discrete but interacting levels—what Simon calls "nearly-decomposable" levels. Simon and Grobstein begin with the modified Chinese boxes model of collections within collections, which is an extension of the levels concept to three dimensions or n dimensions. But what generates these levels? Why are the levels discrete? What separates the levels? What couples the levels together? This is the more significant type of question all the authors have tried to approach.

Simon explains or justifies the origin of levels in two ways. First, he argues that the speed of evolution of complex systems will favor those with stable, intermediate *levels of structure.* A difficult construction is easier to accomplish if done in stages. His second argument does not have to do with actually building a complex system; rather, it deals with describing it. Here his point is that complex systems are incomprehensible unless we simplify them by using alternative *levels of description*. His main example is the operation of a computer, which requires several levels of description to program effectively.

Grobstein bases his concept of hierarchy on the developmental process in living organisms. He sees the levels generated by the collective interaction of elementary structures. The transition from the elements to the collection he calls a context change. The structures generated by one set of elements and their interactions become reinterpreted or re-read in the context of a larger set of interactions to form a higher level. Grobstein illustrates this transition by the folding of a linear chain of amino acid residues into a three-dimensional, functioning enzyme, where the new interactions produced by the folding of the chain give a new context to the initial set of amino acids. This folding process is both obvious and mysterious—it is obvious in the structural context, where each interaction is ordinary physics and chemistry, and mysterious in the functional context, which has only been achieved by unknown spans of evolutionary interactions at even higher levels of organization. In any case, Grobstein's basic observation is that the elements of the organization at any level are not limited by their inherent *structural* and interactional properties at that level, but may generate "emergent" properties in the *new context* of a larger set.

Bonner also bases his discussion of hierarchy on the developmental process in living organisms, but he has found it instructive to go beyond the analytical process of isolating the chemicals that control various developmental stages, and ask the synthetic question, "If I were a cell, what control information would I need to produce this organism?" Bonner finds that he cannot imitate the developmental process without levels of alternative subroutines as well as levels of tests for choosing which alternative subroutine to use at a given stage of development. There must be a detailed description within the subroutine level as well as a higher level description of the various subroutines that are "called" according to the results of the developmental tests. In other words, like Simon's computer program, Bonner finds that the actual construction of the multicellular organism from a single cell requires several *levels of description* in its genetic instructions.

In my own chapter I take up the problem of hierarchical control at the prebiological level. I ask what physical meaning we can attach to molecules that also serve as messages selectively controlling the rates of alternative events. I find that physical description runs into the same problems as Grobstein's biological description—that molecules have no inherent message, but that message behavior emerges only in the new context of a larger set of constraints. Furthermore, like Simon and Bonner, I find even in physics the transitions to a new context—from the dynamical level to the statistical level, from the statistical level to the constraint level, and from the constraint level to the measurement or control level —all require *alternative levels of description.*

Levins takes up the problem of the limits of complexity at the other extreme of the biological hierarchy—that is, at the ecological and evolutionary level. His basic argument is that very complex systems are dominated by processes that are self-simplifying. While Simon's point is that complex systems are incomprehensible unless we choose alternative descriptions that selectively ignore detail, Levins argues that complex systems actually tend to persist only in simplified modes of behavior. Levins illustrates this suggestion by the behavior of Kauffman's randomly connected, random switching networks. These are networks of n switches with two inputs per switch, which have the possibility of passing through 2^n states, but which spontaneously simplify their persistent behavior to approximately $\sqrt{n}$ states—an enormous simplification for large n. Levins further argues that partial decomposability is an *objective* trait of natural selection in complex systems, so that we do not have to view hierarchical organizations as generated from simple components that evolve greater and greater complexity. Instead we may think of hierarchical constraints as *self-simplifications* of initially chaotic, very complex systems (cf. Pattee, 1971). The detailed level of description of the original complex system must then be augmented with an alternative simplified description of the new level.

The common theme characterizing hierarchical systems in these papers that I believe should be emphasized is the double requirement of *levels of description* as well as the more obvious requirement of *levels of structure.* Where there is still a fundamental question—and a wide range of attitudes—is in *the origin and relation of the structural and descriptional levels.* At one extreme there is the view that the laws of nature are entirely objective and determine the structural levels of matter; e.g., particles, atoms, molecules, cells, organisms, etc., which we, as outside observers, find it convenient to analyze by adopting corresponding levels of description. At the other extreme there is the view that whatever the underlying "objective" reality may be, what we understand by laws of nature are structured by the levels of description we choose, and in the context of which we formulate the design and results of our observations.

The Central Problem of Hierarchy Theory

My own view is that *the relation between the structural and descriptive levels is the central problem* that must be solved to have a theory of hierarchical control. The relation of the structure of the physical world and our observation and description of the world is also the central and profound problem of epistemology, which is normally associated with the philosophy of science rather than the practice of science and its technological applications. One may well ask then, if such questions are important for the very practical aim for which we expect any theory of hierarchical organizations to be useful—that is, the design and management of complex social and technological systems. At first thought, the epistemological relation between events and descriptions of events—between matter and symbol—might appear largely irrelevant to the problem of programming a computer or managing a factory or an ecosystem. Would we ever seriously evaluate a computer programmer or manager by asking if he is a naive realist or a solipsist? Of course not—at least not in this philosophical context. On the other hand, would we seriously consider hiring a computer programmer who did not have a practical understanding of the difference between hardware and software—that is, between the physical structures of the computer and the descriptive structures by which the programmer controls the computer? We would indeed be upset if we found a programmer who began rewiring the computer circuits the first time his program did not work! On the other hand, he should know that there is always the possibility that the structure of the computer could fail in such a way that no amount of reprogramming could correct the problem. For the same reason we would be skeptical of a new production manager whose first recommendation was to rebuild the factory, although again in rare cases this may be the best alternative. My point is that the manager of any complex organization must clearly appreciate the distinction between the structural levels and the descriptive levels of the system and must know how they interact. He must recognize the difference between a descriptive failure and a structural failure; he must know which levels are dominant and which are subordinate; and he must know when new structural and descriptive levels are needed. Otherwise, even though he is called the manager of the system, he may not have control over it. This we know from experience is often the case with administrators of large social, business, and political organizations.

The primary reason that the modern computer is both a practical machine as well as a useful analogy for other complex organizations is because there is both a clear separation between its structural and descriptive levels—between its hardware and software—as well as a clear understanding of their relationships. The computer hardware is designed with the express purpose of being entirely subordinate to its instructions. One might say that it is one of the purer forms of hierarchical organization, where there is supposed to be absolutely no doubt about where the authority lies or in how the levels are to interact with each other.

However, for all this artificial purity in its hierarchical organization, the largest computers are still no match for natural, biological organizations, especially in those tasks that require creative design, description, and organization. The purity of the artificial levels seems to limit its efficiency. Much of the program of the living organism can now be recognized in the sequence of bases in the DNA molecule of the gene. The sequence of amino acid residues in all the enzymes is known to be subordinate to this sequence of bases, but beyond this, the levels of authority become much more difficult to establish, since the organism lives autonomously as a more or less closed network of control levels. Following Bonner we can say that the expression of the genetic subroutines are controlled by the developmental tests. But by what authority are these tests chosen, described and coordinated? What determines when a new level of structures, descriptions and tests are necessary? What determines the immediate goals or the life-span of the whole organism? What determines the authority levels within a society of organisms? To answer this type of question we need to know how structural and descriptive levels interact. It is not generally the case, in living systems, as it is in the computer, that the descriptive levels dominate the structural levels. The developmental process clearly subordinates the description (i.e., what is expressed) to the organism structure. Similarly the outside environment may at certain times in the life cycle dominate the internal descriptions.

Extreme Examples of Structure-Description Relationships

The word hierarchy is often applied to ranks or levels of either physical or symbolic structure alone. For example, the sizes of objects from atoms to nebulae can serve as a levels structure (e.g., see Wilson, 1969); or the sizes of symbol structures from letters to paragraphs produce a ranked ordering which can be called hierarchical (e.g., see Whyte, 1969). However, as each author here has made clear in his own way, this somewhat trivial usage of the concept of hierarchy is not of particular interest in the context of a theory of design and control of complex systems. To restate what we said before, to be able to rationally design and control complex organizations will require a deeper understanding of the coupling between physical and symbolic structures—that is, between events and descriptions of events.

It is instructive to look at extreme examples of structural and descriptive interactions. In what type of system do we treat the structure as entirely autonomous and the description as entirely subordinate? Classical concepts of mechanics come very close to this extreme. Space, time, and matter for Newton were absolute structures that had very little to do with their description—so little, in fact, that the interactions of the structure of nature with the description of nature were hardly recognized as a problem. Two centuries later, Hertz clearly recognized the problem in his mechanics, and attempted to clarify it with the requirement of the structure-description parallelism; that is, the requirement that the necessary consequences of our descriptions must result in images of nature that are the necessary consequences of the events of nature itself. He also saw that elements of our descriptions could be empty or arbitrary without making the description false, and that the structure of nature did not determine our description of nature unambiguously. Besides parallelism, the only other requirement of the description was that it be perfectly clear and unambiguous in its internal consequences. In any case, we may use the ideal classical picture of nature as an example of structure that was assumed to be largely isolated from its description, and certainly in absolutely no sense influenced or controlled by any description. Dynamical systems theory is essentially an outgrowth of this classical picture of nature.

What example can we find at the other extreme? Are there systems whose structures are entirely subordinate to their descriptions? I would say that an ideal computer would satisfy this requirement. Real computers are designed with this ideal in mind, but obviously cannot achieve the ideal because the structural components are always "limited" in some way by the laws of nature; their size, speed, reliability, for example, are not entirely under descriptive control. Nevertheless, when we program computers or think about the computer as a model or analogue, we cannot at the same time describe its physical structure. That is, in programming we must ignore the physical structure to get logical results. The computer is supposed to do only what we instruct it to do no matter what its structure happens to be. We can imagine, then, at one extreme, the ideal classical "mechanism" that we can describe completely, but over which the description has no influence, and at the other extreme, the ideal computer "mechanism" that we never describe completely but over which we have complete descriptive control.

This contrast can be carried even deeper. We know that the ideal determinism of classical physics is only an approximation that holds for very large objects. In quantum dynamics we find that although we assume a complete mathematical description of the time evolution of pure states that is formally exact and deterministic, it is nevertheless physically impossible to actually measure or control the state of a system with absolute precision. There is the well-known Heisenberg *uncertainty principle,* which expresses the fundamental indeterminism in any attempt to control all the variables defining the state at a given instant of time. On the other hand, we find that purely symbolic or logical systems that are rich enough to allow self-reference (i.e., possessing at least two levels of description) have an essential *incompleteness,* as shown by Gödel. That is, even though the symbols and operations of logic are completely precise and deterministic, there are many types of problems that are unsolvable. For example, there can be no general algorithm for predicting whether a computer will halt, even though the computation is precisely defined.

Therefore, we have the following extreme pictures: On the one hand, there is the very simple quantum mechanical system for which we assume a complete dynamical description in time, but which exhibits a necessary indeterminism when we attempt to observe or control it. On the other hand, we have symbolic logical systems for which we assume precise deterministic operations under our control, but which exhibit incomplete and unpredictable behavior when we try to solve certain types of computational problems. We might say that sufficiently simple natural structures are predictable but uncontrollable, whereas sufficiently complex symbolic descriptions are controllable but unpredictable.

Thoughts on the Root of the Problem

Real hierarchical systems fall in between these two extremes in the relation between their structural and dynamical levels, but I chose these extreme cases to illustrate the principle difficulty in relating structure and description—or as I have expressed it alternatively, the difficulty in relating *pre-*

diction of how a system behaves and *control* of how it behaves. These pairs of concepts—structure and description, prediction and control—are particular examples of hierarchical concepts which have meaning on two different levels. The important point to realize is that all forms of management or control must operate between two hierarchical levels. This is true for any informational constraints where structural alternatives on one level are subordinated by a higher level descriptive process. This is the case in all forms of decision-making, classification, recognition, or measurement process.

Why is this so? Why are two levels of structure and description necessary for any prediction and control process? The basic reason is that in order to predict how a system will behave we must assume it can behave only one way, according to its dynamical law, without the possibility of some alternative behavior. On the other hand, in order to speak of controlling a system we must assume that alternative behaviors are possible. How can a system have control alternatives when no dynamical alternatives exist? This is the same conceptual problem that has troubled physicists for so long with respect to irreversibility. How can a dynamical system governed deterministically by time-symmetric equations of motion exhibit irreversible behavior? And of course there is the same conceptual difficulty in the old problem of free will—how can we be governed by inexorable natural laws and still choose to do whatever we wish? These questions appear paradoxical only in the context of single-level descriptions. If we assume one dynamical law of motion that is time-reversible, then there is no way that elaborating more and more complex systems will produce irreversibility under this single dynamical description. I strongly suspect that this simple fact is at the root of the measurement problem in quantum theory, in which the reversible dynamical laws cannot be used to describe the measurement process. If the event itself is time-symmetric, then the record of the event cannot be, for it is primarily by records that we give time a direction. This argument is also very closely related to the logician's argument that any description of the truth of a symbolic statement must be in a richer metalanguage (i.e., more alternatives) than the language in which the proposition itself is stated.

More Concrete Examples of the Problem

But now I am straying from the practical questions of the relation of the structural to the descriptive levels. Let us grant that hierarchical control theory must recognize the necessity of alternative levels of description—all the authors have stressed this point. What has happened to the corresponding structural levels? In my own discussion I have lapsed into the common assumption of a disembodied language or symbol system as a basis for my levels of description. We operate with our own natural language as if it needed no structural basis whatever, and when we speak of other types of symbol systems we usually carry over this unjustified abstraction.

It is because we commonly fail to recognize the nature of the necessary structural basis of symbol vehicles and grammatical constraints that the use of biological organisms and computers as models of hierarchical organizations is so helpful. The perspective of modern biology is entirely structure-oriented—so much so, in fact, that the essential symbolic aspects of life are often missed. DNA is certainly a description, but to most biologists today, DNA is first and foremost a structure. Similarly the genetic code reads and constructs enzymes from this description, but no one imagines these interactions outside the framework of the message and transfer RNA molecules, the coding enzymes, and the ribosomal structures, which actually execute these symbol-manipulating and translating processes. And even when we discuss higher level descriptions—for example, Bonner's developmental subroutines and their tests and transfer commands—there is no doubt that each symbol and operation exists in the cell as a specific molecule or structure. The computer analogy is particularly useful (cf. Simon, p. 12) simply because the levels of structure and levels of description are kept cleanly separated, while at the same time there is no mystery as to what structure corresponds to what symbol or description. However, the computer analogy is not accurate, and this inaccuracy may be a fundamental problem for modeling biological hierarchies. The analogy breaks down because biological structures are grown continuously under the instructions of the genetic program, whereas the structure of computers is relatively fixed. Biological organizations can therefore build new structures from new descriptions, and undoubtedly the richness of the hierarchical levels in living systems depends to some degree on this special ability; but again we have no idea of the processes that generate new levels.

Theories of Origin of Levels—Instabilities and Catastrophes

How do new levels of hierarchical organization arise spontaneously? How do new structures appear without pre-existing descriptions? This is a fundamental problem for hierarchy theory at all levels. In living organisms it is no exaggeration to say that the genetic code establishes the most fundamental interaction between the descriptive and structural levels, and yet in spite of a rather detailed knowledge of how the code operates, we are still at a loss to understand how the code originated. At the other end of the evolutionary spectrum, we are now beginning to understand the fundamental levels of language systems, but again we have almost no idea of the origin of these levels. We have learned from our experience with building and managing complex organizations that when the complexity of any level grows beyond a certain range, function becomes impaired, operation becomes inefficient, and reliability declines. We know that *ad hoc* corrections and local improvements in efficiency can only go so far in correcting the problems, and that sooner or later we must face a total "reorganization" of the system that must essentially alter the hierarchical control and levels structure. But beyond our traditional empirical knowledge of how such organizations have been run in the past, we are at a loss to design any part of a rational hierarchical structure from theoretical principles.

Levin's paper suggests a theoretical basis for the self-simplification or "clustering" of interactions that would appear as a new hierarchical level; but he assumes an initial complexity that allows natural selection. There are, however, several other theories or approaches to the origin of more elementary physical levels of organization which may turn out to have sufficient depth to qualify for a general theory of hierarchical origins. To conclude this postscript I will try to summarize these approaches and suggest a few possible directions for further development and application.

It is a common observation that the regular dynamical behavior of simple physical systems may suddenly lapse into an entirely new pattern of activity—a spinning top will suddenly fall over, a shade will begin to flap in the wind, or a smooth wave will break into white crests. In dynamical language these sudden changes of pattern we attribute to instabilities. In simple mechanical systems the concept of stability can be clearly defined in terms of the system's ability to return to its original type of trajectory after being transiently perturbed. In a good dynamical theory, the regions of physical instability can be predicted since they correspond to singularities in the mathematical description. But very often the behavior of the system beyond its stable regime is not predictable or even describable in terms of the lower level dynamics. We have an example, then, of a new level of structure and a new level of description arising from instability.

It is important to distinguish this spontaneous generation of a new hierarchical level from the use of new descriptive levels alone. For example, the slow diffusion of dye molecules in a solution can be clearly described in terms of a new concentration variable, but is extremely difficult to describe in terms of the detailed motion of the individual molecules. In this case, however, the motion of the individual molecules is in no way altered or subordinated to the new description using concentration as a variable. In other words, we have levels of description, and if we wish, levels of structure, but no *new* subordination or dominance relations among any of these levels of structure or description. On the other hand, when instabilities occur, the collective motions or patterns act as new constraints on the individual elements and therefore can be said to exercise a dominant effect on their behavior. For example, when we say the flow of molecules in a gas forms a whirlwind, we have more than an alternative description; we have a new structure which dominates the motion of individual molecules. We can say a new hierarchical level has been formed.

The question is how far this process of creation of new levels by instabilities applies to more complex systems. Unfortunately, the very concept of stability loses its clarity as the systems grow in complexity. Furthermore, the theory of dynamical stability is well developed only for local regions of the trajectories, and what any hierarchical theory must recognize is the global stability of the system. Nevertheless, the further study of the behavior of instabilities and singularities in dynamical systems is one of the most promising directions that hierarchy theory should take. This approach has been advanced by Prigogine and his coworkers who have specialized in the description of thermodynamic instabilities far from equilibrium where there is high dissipation and non-linearity. He views the levels of biological hierarchies as closely related to a succession of instabilities (Prigogine and Nicolis, 1971; Glansdorff and Prigogine, 1971).

A more general mathematical approach to the origin of structure through instabilities is Thom's theory of catastrophes, which is based on the concept of structural stability in topological dynamics (Thom, 1970). Thom would not call this a theory of hierarchies, but rather a method for improving our thinking about complex systems—"an art of models." I would agree that we should not expect early advances in our understanding of hierarchical origins to be found in quantitative mathematical models or in new formalisms. We are still too far from a conceptual appreciation—too far from even an intuitive picture—of hierarchical complexity. No hierarchy theory will be of much value if it is expressed in a mathematical formalism that is itself of comparable complexity to the systems it is describing. The essence of a good theory of complex systems will tell us how to make them simpler.

Hierarchy Theory and Systems Theory

How would we expect a theory of hierarchies to differ from the well-established dynamical systems theory and control theory? To what extent should we try to carry over the basic techniques and formalism of systems theory to hierarchies? The dynamical language with its concepts of states, observables, and equations of motion is so general and has proven so useful that it is not likely to be entirely replaced. Nevertheless, dynamical theories are all single-level theories—in one sense a dynamics defines what we call a level. We can use the dynamical language on as many levels as we wish, because we may choose our state variables in almost any way we wish, but for this reason we lose the essential relations between levels. Dynamical theory artificially separates levels by allowing us an unrestricted choice of state variables. The problem of relating the variables on two levels is usually left as a special exercise in interpretation independent of the dynamics at either level. One central aim of control in dynamical systems is to avoid instabilities at all costs, since instability generally leads to a new dynamical regime. A second common goal in control theory is to optimize certain parameters under a given set of fixed constraints. Many of the mathematical techniques of dynamical and control theory have been stimulated by these goals (e.g., see Bellman and Kalaba, 1964).

In terms of structural and descriptive levels, we may look at dynamical formalism as a universal description which, because of its universality, has nothing to do with the particular structure it is describing, other than maintaining the essential Hertzian parallelism; i.e., the consequences of the description must describe the consequences of the natural events. This is the basis of the so-called dynamical analogy which is of great value (e.g., see Rosen, 1970). But this is the same kind of purity we found in the computer program or software, which has nothing to do with the actual structure of the switches and wires of the computer hardware, other than exerting control over the output symbols. Both dynamics and automata theories, indeed most of mathematics, have been brought to such a state of purity in their descriptive formalisms that hierarchical levels appear totally isolated from each other. Mathematical descriptions therefore tend to create *total* decomposition, whereas the essential behavior of real hierarchical systems depends on the *partial* decomposition of levels, as Simon has emphasized. We find then that dynamical systems theory emphasizes holistic, single-level descriptions, avoidance of instabilities, optimization under fixed constraints and artificial isolation of adjacent levels.

In contrast to systems theory, hierarchy theory must be formulated to describe at least two levels at a time, it must optimize constraints for a given function, and it must allow interactions between alternative levels. Since there is no obvious way to extend the dynamical language to encompass these requirements, perhaps hierarchy theory will require a dualistic or parallel type of theory not unlike the wave-particle duality of quantum physics, where neither description alone is adequate, but where simultaneous use of both appears inconsistent. The essential rules of such a theory would specify under what conditions or for what type of question each description is to be applied.

Hierarchy Theory and Evolution Theory.

Optimization and control must take on a much broader meaning in any theory of hierarchies since all the complex systems we need to control are growing systems. It is not appropriate to consider the constraints as fixed and search for local optima in the parameters. As Levins and I indicated in our chapters, hierarchical control consists largely of optimization of the level of constraints in forming new structural levels and in the optimization of loss of detail in forming new descriptive levels. Also, the theory of hierarchies must be closely related to the theory of evolution. Both must account for the long range behavior of complex, growing systems that have descriptive and structural levels; but while the analogy may be helpful, the theory of evolution itself lacks an independent measure of fitness, without which it has very little predictive value. Therefore, unless we can find better measures of fitness and quality of function we have little hope of achieving any form of optimization in such systems by a theoretical approach. Until we find these measures, tradition and trial and error will continue to be the "method" of hierarchical control as well as evolution.

At this stage in our thinking we are still a long way from a useful theory of complex systems. But our review of the properties of hierarchies offers some suggestions that we may at least use in our explorations or our attempts to control our complex technical, social, or ecological system. First, we should be more cautious in regarding optimization in a systems sense as always a good thing. At least we must be more aware that what is optimized depends on the choice of description. If our description is chosen subjectively or arbitrarily with no necessary integration with the structure it describes, then we have no assurance that the organization as a whole will benefit. An all too common result of attempting to optimize a controllable parameter is to produce an instability that may result in irreversible damage to the organization. On the other hand, a second caution is that not all instabilities should be regarded as a bad thing. While many artificial machines tend to fail if the stable regime of their normal operation is exceeded, natural organizations from cells to ecosystems tend to have many regimes that may be triggered by instabilities. Furthermore, if the theory of organization through instabilities has some truth, then our main effort should be to distinguish those instabilities that are simply disintegrative from those that reintegrate the elements into new levels of organization.

Finally, in hierarchical organizations we should overcome our traditional classical emphasis on the structural levels and recognize the essential role of the descriptive levels in maintaining and coordinating organization. We still put by far our greatest efforts and money into computer hardware, which by now has reached incredible levels of sophistication, rather than into programming theory, which is still in a primitive state. Perhaps for this reason we have not been able to program computers to evolve new levels or model biological evolution in any realistic way. Our preoccupation with the physical and technical aspects of machines has obscured the fact that a failure of description may be more profound and more difficult to correct than a failure of structure. Therefore, along with the study of the hierarchies of biological development, evolution and ecology, physical and mathematical instabilities, and origin processes, the theory of complex systems will also depend on a deeper understanding of descriptive levels and the theory of language.

Hierarchy Theory and Language Theory

As a final suggestion for directions that the study of hierarchy theories may usefully follow, I would return again to the common problem—the relation between structural and descriptive levels; and now I would ask what meanings we can give to the concept of description at the simplest level. If we want to understand the simplest hierarchical organization we must ask, What is the simplest type of description? The normal usage of the word "description" presupposes a human language in which the description is expressed. However, as we have seen, especially from Bonner's paper, we also find it meaningful to speak of the cell's genetic description of itself as well as its description of how to develop into a multicellular organism. Perhaps a linguist would prefer some other word in place of description, such as, prescription or instruction, but that does not touch the root of the problem. Any concept of sign- or symbol-mediated events or behavior presupposes a set of constraints or rules which serve to distinguish the symbols from the events as well as the relation between them. Thus, we call DNA a description only in association with the molecular constraints that make up the genetic code. But in spite of our knowledge of the code and much of its structural embodiment, we have no good theory of its origin or why it has the properties it does. We suspect that much of the structure is arbitrary, just as much of the structural embodiments of human language are arbitrary. Somehow we must find what is essential in both cases. Such an understanding would, in my view, form the foundation of a theory of language as well as the basis for a theory of hierarchies.

I am aware that traditional linguistics would not consider such simple rules as those represented by the genetic code as an example of language. Most linguistic studies tend to define away the problems of origin and evolution of language by refusing to accept non-human symbol systems as language. While this is no place to consider such a difficult matter of definition, it is at least clear that the descriptive potential of the genetic code is rich enough to actually construct in each individual those hierarchical constraints which support language at whatever level one chooses to define the concept. In other words, the descriptive function established by the genetic code, in spite of its apparent simplicity, does not have any obvious limitations in its potential for generating complex hierarchical organizations and functions. Human languages share this apparently unlimited potential for generating complex levels of meanings, but unlike the code, human language is so complicated that as yet we have no clear understanding of the basic elements and rules that are necessary to support these higher languages.

What I suggest therefore, is to study the simplest possible language-like structures or, if you prefer, descriptive processes, that can create a clear separation of hierarchical levels. The genetic code system is much simpler than human language, and yet it is already too complex to understand how it began. Can we imagine simpler rules and relations that allow matter to operate as symbolic representations? Clearly, such simple descriptive systems will not exhibit the range of capabilities of higher language, but at least we should find in such examples a clearer picture of what the physical requirements are for any symbolic activity to arise in matter. Physical theories are created to describe the simplest imaginable systems; for example, the mass point, the hydrogen atom, the equilibrium gas, or the plane wave. The choice of theories also depends strongly on very abstract principles of conservation, symmetry, invariance, or impotence. From these elementary theories we build up descriptions of more and more complex systems. But in all these efforts we take for granted that we may use any language we wish and as many as necessary. That is, we choose whatever mathematical formalism is most useful and then interpret the symbols and measurement operations in very highly developed natural language. To a large degree, the simplicity of natural laws arises through the complexities of the languages we use for their expression. (cf. Wigner, 1959).

Perhaps we will find that just as no elementary descriptive systems such as nucleic acids and their transcribing and constructing enzymes are designed to directly formulate high-level symbolic concepts such as symmetry or conservation, so neither are our theories of simple physical systems designed to directly explain a description of even the most elementary symbolic processes. The genetic code as it now exists might suggest that there is a threshold of physical complexity below which no meaning can be attached to a description; that is, below this level we would only recognize physical interactions with no internal symbolic aspects. A similar suggestion was made by von Neumann (1966) in considering the logical design of a self-reproducing automaton which required an internal description. One can also see that some threshold of complexity of language is necessary to formulate what we would call even the simplest physical law. It is at this level of interplay between the most elementary descriptive activity and the physical systems that they constrain, that there may be some hope of discovering a deeper relation between the parts and wholes of hierarchies.

REFERENCES

Bellman, R. and Kalaba, R. 1964. *Selected Papers on Mathematical Trends in Control Theory.* New York: Dover Publications.

Glansdorff, P. and Prigogine, I. 1971. *Thermodynamic Theory of Structure, Stability and Fluctuations.* London: Wiley-Interscience.

Pattee, H. H. 1971. The recognition of description and function in chemical reaction networks. *Molecular Evolution.* Buvet, R. and Ponnamperuma, C., eds. p. 42. Amsterdam: North Holland Pub. Co.

Prigogine, I. and Nicolis, G. 1971. Biological order, structure and instabilities. *Quarterly Review of Biophysics 4,* 107.

Rosen, R. 1970. *Dynamical Systems Theory in Biology.* New York: Wiley-Interscience.

Thom, R. 1970. Topological models in biology. *Towards a Theoretical Biology 3: Drafts,* C. H. Waddington, ed. p. 89. University of Edinburgh Press.

von Neumann, J. 1966. *Theory of Self-Reproducing Automata,* Burks, A. W., ed., Univ. Ill. Press, Urbana.

Whyte, L. L. 1969. Structural hierarchies: a challenging class of biological and physical problems. *Hierarchical Structures,* Whyte, L. L., Wilson, A. G., and Wilson, D., eds. p. 3. New York: American Elsevier.

Wigner, E. P. 1959. The unreasonable effectiveness of mathematics in the natural sciences. *Communications on Pure and Applied Math. 13,* 1.

Wilson, A. G. 1969. Hierarchical structures in the cosmos. *Hierarchical Structures,* Whyte, L. L., Wilson, A. G., and Wilson, D., eds. p. 113. New York: American Elsevier.